THE OAKWOOD PRESS

CW00663804

Isle of Wight Here We Come

The Story of the Southern Railway's Isle of Wight Ships During the War 1939-1945

by
Hugh J. Compton

THE OAKWOOD PRESS

© Oakwood Press & Hugh J. Compton 1997

British Library Cataloguing in Publication Data
A Record for this book is available from the British Library
ISBN 0 85361 506 3

Typeset by Oakwood Graphics.
Repro by Ford Graphics, Ringwood, Hants.
Printed by The Witney Press, Witney, Oxon.

PS Sandown in naval role June 1940
Summer in the seas off Dover may seem warm, but some of the ship's crew are certainly clothed against the elements whilst keeping an eye out for 'E' boats and enemy aircraft.
Portsmouth Record Office

Front cover: PS *Merstone* arriving at Ryde. *E.W. Paget-Tomlinson*
Rear cover, top: Lymington Pier station is seen here on a typical summer's day in the immediate post-War period. A tank engine runs round its train whilst a car is driven off MV *Lymington* and PS *Freshwater* sets off for Yarmouth IOW. *F. Burridge*
Rear cover, bottom: A Southern Railway poster promoting the Isle of Wight.
National Railway Museum/Science & Society

Published by
The Oakwood Press
P.O. Box 122, Headington, Oxford, OX3 8LU.

Contents

PS Ryde on cruise round the Isle of Wight, 1939
Before the War the Southern Railway operated excursions from both Portsmouth and Ryde round the Isle of Wight. This was very popular and enabled the boats to be used when not engaged on the heavy weekend commitments. However, when working around the Island their passage certificate was somewhat reduced. The service was withdrawn just before the outbreak of War, when ships were required for the evacuation of children from Portsmouth to the Isle of Wight.   *Frank Burridge*

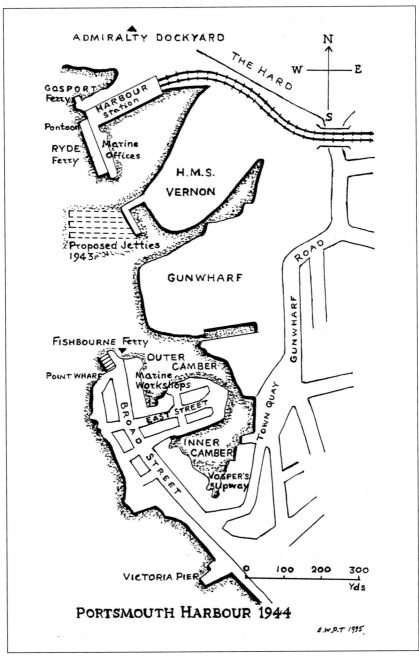

Map of Portsmouth Harbour, 1944.   *E.W. Paget-Tomlinson*

Acknowledgements

The writing of this book could not have been done without the help of those who were actually there, in particular Eddie Morgan, Ray Butcher and Fred Howland of the Southern Railway's Docks and Marine Dept. My researching through the RAIL collection at the Public Record Office, Kew and the voluminous collection at the British Railways Board Record Centre has been helped immensely by Robin Linsley and Richard Wood and their staff. My debt is due also to the staff at the Public Record Office, Kew, who kindly made available for my inspection well over 100 files deposited there by the Admiralty and the War Office. Libraries too have played their part, in particular those at Southampton, Lymington, Cowes, Newport, Ryde and Portsmouth. Many people have gone out of their way to help, especially Miss Sherwood of the Portsmouth Museum, who generously allowed me to make extracts from her unpublished MS entitled 'The House at the Point'. The Lymington route chapter would not have been possible without the aid given by Alan Brown and Ben Wales. For the colourful artwork I am happy to record my thanks to Edward Paget-Tomlinson and Frank Burridge. Last and by no means least, I am grateful to the many members of the Railway & Canal Historical Society who not only provided information but also helped with the final preparation of this work. Finally, it is hoped that this book will provide a fitting remembrance to all those who by tireless work and endurance under what must have been very trying circumstances enabled the Southern Railway to maintain its link with the Isle of Wight throughout the War.

The Author

Following education at King's Bruton and a spell in the Army, he joined the Southern Region of British Railways on nationalisation. Thereafter he was involved in a number of projects including the electrification of the Isle of Wight Railways. Since retirement at middle management level he has continued his interest in transport history and is now the London Group Chairman of the Railway & Canal Historical Society.

Before the War the railways operated a number of air services to the Isle of Wight to prevent competition. This poster shows an aircraft coming into Ryde airport from Heston (London). The service was withdrawn before the War.

National Railway Museum/Science & Society

Chapter One

The Overall Picture

Many people can still recall the joy of crossing to/from the Isle of Wight (IOW) under a sunny sky with a light breeze blowing, on one of those delightful little ships owned by the Southern Railway. All this suddenly changed when on 3rd September, 1939 the Government assumed control of the railways under Defence Regulation No. 69, though this did not affect all the services to the Island, as the Southampton, Isle of Wight and South of England Royal Mail Steam Packet Co. (Red Funnel) operated between Southampton and Cowes for both freight and passengers. In addition, Messrs Pickford operated a freight service with barges from Portsmouth (Point Wharf) to Cowes (Thetis Wharf), which was excluded.

At that time the SR had 13 ships to cover the three routes between the mainland and the IOW, these being built between 1902 and 1937 with a variety in design, propulsion and carrying capacity. In the main, the passenger business had to be geared up to deal with the six week peak season in the summer, while the freight and vehicular movement was more evenly spread. There was one other vessel which was stationed at Portsmouth, and which, though small, nevertheless performed a very useful function. This was the motor boat called *Alice*, which was built by Vosper's of Broad Street, Portsmouth in 1926. She was used to transport crews from the pontoon by the Harbour station to the ships berthed alongside the coal hulk, to run the mooring ropes to the buoy for the car ferries to moor astern of the coal hulk overnight. In addition she helped move staff and stores from the Marine workshops to the ships as well as transport the catering stores. One job which took her out of Portsmouth harbour was to go every so often to Fishbourne and refill the gas cylinders on the dolphins there. Bad weather gave her extra work too when she was called upon to double as a tug and assist by holding the car ferries into the wind. Sometimes she had to help the paddle steamers in the same way. Small she may have been, but nevertheless useful.

Unlike the cross-channel fleet, these vessels on the IOW working had up to three sets of crews to cover sailings over a 24-hour period. However, during the off-season, when the ships' officers were retained irrespective of traffic needs, other members of the crew were not so fortunate, being generally laid off. Another distinction as compared with their cross-channel colleagues` that became apparent shortly after the declaration of War, was that the special war allowance paid to men on the channel fleet in recognition of their having to work in a dangerous area, was denied to those on the IOW ships. Perhaps the fact that they only worked in our territorial waters had something to do with this decision. The services from Portsmouth to both Ryde and Fishbourne were directed by C.T. Pelly, Divisional Marine Manager from his office at 102 Broad Street, Portsmouth, whilst those for the Lymington-Yarmouth route came under the direct control of the Docks and Marine Manager's Office in Canute Road, Southampton, though after August 1940 the office moved to Embley Park, Romsey. In addition to his operating duties, Mr Pelly had a small self-contained workshop which could perform any task not requiring dry-docking. The staff of this establishment was as under:

PS Sandown at Southampton November 1939
The stern view of PS *Sandown* following her conversion for the Navy clearly shows her mine-sweeping equipment where formerly there had been a passenger lounge with rows of seats above. The 'Oropesa' sweep was trailed at the end of a sweep wire which cut the mooring wires of mines.   *F. Hawkes*

Foreman	1	Shipwright	1	Fitters	4
Blacksmith	1	Painter	1	Labourers	2
Plumber	1	Storekeeper	1		
Joiner	1	Boatman	1	TOTAL	14

As these vessels were designed for working in the Solent/Spithead area one would not expect to find them elsewhere, but on occasions they were used on mid-week excursions to Sandown and Shanklin with occasional trips around the IOW and also to Bournemouth. Indeed, it is surprising to find that some of those which were requisitioned got far away from their normal sphere of operation, but with their limited bunkers, coal stocks had to be replenished at the end of two days from the coal hulk, and fuel oil after three days. From time to time the coal hulk had to be taken to the SR jetty in the Dockyard for replenishment of its coal supply direct from wagons.

In the early days of the War the dropping of magnetic mines in shallow waters by the German Air Force caused heavy losses of shipping. The magnetic mine is so called, not because it is attracted to the ship's hull, but because it is detonated by a magnetic needle which becomes active when a large mass of iron passes through its field. When the mine is laid on the sea bottom it can operate only in comparatively shallow water, but within its range it can cause far more damage than the moored mine, since the moored mine blows a hole in the ship, usually forward, which may be localised, whereas the explosion from a ground mine strikes the vessel amidships, opening the plates of the hull, shattering the machinery and the pipes, and frequently breaking her back. To counter the magnetic mine ships were provided with a simple but effective device known as a 'degaussing girdle' which could be fitted to vessels of any size. This consisted of a band of wire fastened round the hull, level with the upper deck and energised by an electric current, which had the effect of neutralising the ship's magnetism and giving her almost complete immunity. The necessary work was undertaken either in the Naval dockyard at Portsmouth or in the docks at Southampton. The overall cost per ship was in the order of £1,000, but as revealed in the SR's General Manager's Conference on 20th March, 1940, the railway paid only between £50 and £100 per ship, the remainder being paid by the Government. However, the work could not be carried out until after the Naval and requisitioned ships had been so equipped. Thus ships which belonged to the SR's IOW fleet were not protected till after Dunkirk.

Following the withdrawal of our forces from the mainland of Europe in May/June 1940, it seemed probable that as a first step the Germans might actually carry out an invasion of the Isle of Wight prior to landing on the English mainland. Indeed, on 13th July Field Marshal von Brauchitsch and General Halder had conferred with Hitler at the Berghof, his mountain retreat near Salzburg, on this very matter. Directive 16 issued afterwards stated that 'consideration was to be given to a surprise crossing on a broad front from Ramsgate to a point west of the Isle of Wight, and also to the advantages of preliminary operations such as the occupation of the Isle of Wight before the full-scale invasion'. The Ministry of Home Security had already taken this probability into account by issuing an order under Defence (General) Regulation

DIRECTIONS OF THE REGIONAL COMMISSIONER UNDER REGULATION 16A OF THE DEFENCE (GENERAL) REGULATIONS, 1939.

No. 84

I, in exercise of the powers conferred upon me by Regulation 16A of the Defence (General) Regulations, 1939, hereby make the following Directions :—

1. No person who is not ordinarily resident in the area described in the Schedule hereto shall enter that area, or, having entered it, remain therein :—

    (a) for the purpose of holiday, recreation or pleasure ;

    (b) for the purpose of treatment, or convalescence during or after illness, except as a patient at an approved institution or as a tubercular patient at a sanatorium ;

    (c) as a casual wayfarer :

Provided that this Direction shall not preclude a person from visiting a spouse, parent or child, or a sick or aged near relative, or a relative or friend who is a patient expressly mentioned in sub-paragraph (b) of this Direction, or from attending the wedding or funeral of a relative.

2. No person :—

    (i) who has not resided in the said area between the first day of January, 1939, and the fourteenth day of November, 1941, for periods amounting in the aggregate to six months shall take up residence therein, or

    (ii) who has taken up residence in the said area after the fourteenth day of November, 1941, shall remain in residence therein,

except for the purpose of :

    (a) business or employment or of acting as housekeeper to, or having the care of, a near relative ; or

    (b) residing in premises of which he was on the fourteenth day of November, the owner or the tenant under a lease or tenancy agreement granted or entered into for a term of not less than three years ; or

    (c) residing with a person who is permitted to reside in the said area, provided that he is ordinarily a member of the household of that person ; or

    (d) residing with relatives or friends ; provided that he is the holder of a certificate issued by a local authority relating to the Government evacuation scheme or a certificate issued by a local authority that he has been rendered homeless as a result of enemy action ; or

    (e) treatment or convalescence during or after illness as a patient at an approved institution or as a tubercular patient at a sanatorium.

3. In these Directions the expression " approved institution " means :

    (i) a hospital, clinic, dispensary or convalescent home provided by a local authority or supported wholly or partly out of public funds or by a charity or by voluntary subscriptions ; or

    (ii) any nursing home registered under part VI of the Public Health Act, 1936,

    being an institution established before the 15th April, 1942, or for the establishment of which, arrangements had been made before that date, and approved for the purpose of these directions by the Regional Commissioner.

4. These Directions shall come into force on the 1st October, 1942, and the Directions No. 75 made on the 3rd April, 1942, are hereby revoked.

H. G. HAIG,

Regional Commissioner for the Southern Civil Defence Region.

SOUTHERN REGIONAL HEADQUARTERS,

22nd September, 1942.

SCHEDULE.

The Administrative County of the Isle of Wight.

(12118) Wt. 29681—586 1500 9/42 D.L. G. 373.

16A on 5th July declaring that the Isle of Wight and Portsmouth was a defence area. The SR quickly followed this up with a detailed instruction entitled 'Active Operations in the Isle of Wight', for full details see *Appendix One*.

Hitler's designs on the Island were encapsulated in the film made on the island of Herm in September 1940 entitled *Die Begetzung der Insul Wight* which received an enthusiastic response when shown in Berlin. Who knows what part the SR ferries would have played if this had come about! The railway management could foresee that with the Germans so much closer there was now a very real chance that their IOW ships would soon be receiving unwelcome attention from the Luftwaffe, so the decision was taken to enclose the bridge on each ship in a concrete casing, which was not removed until after the cessation of hostilities, and also to provide them with the minimum of anti-aircraft defence in the form of a Lewis gun.

Without holidaymakers, the services were slimmed down to cater for the Island's population of about 90,000 persons, but to this figure must be added the Island's normal military garrison of about 8,000 men, though just prior to the raid on Dieppe in May 1942 this had risen to 21,668 personnel.

As the war progressed further restrictions on the movement of civilians to and from the Island were issued on 6th November, 1941 and 15th April, 1942, culminating with the comprehensive regulation No. 84 dated 22nd September, 1942 (*see Appendix Two*). Whilst this regulation would appear to take into account all situations, the military became quite concerned on the run up to the Dieppe raid as it seemed some people were able to make the passage by resorting to persuasive conversation with the Ferry Security Police, three of whom had been appointed by the Sea Control Office to monitor these movements. It could also be done by getting someone else to create a diversion while people slipped through. Eventually on 1st January, 1943 a total ban on the movement of civilians was imposed which lasted till after the Dieppe raid. During this period passage could only be made by civilians with the written approval of the Chief Constable of Hampshire. Those in the Armed Services had to obtain proper identity papers issued for 'Operation Rutter' and personally approved by Major-General J.H. Roberts, CB, DSO, MC, Commander of the 2nd Canadian Division and Military Force Commander, or Rear-Admiral H.T. Baillie-Grohman, CB, DSO, OBE, Naval Force Commander.

Shortly after the successful invasion of Normandy the restriction on travelling on the Isle of Wight Ferries was lifted, but persons wishing to land on the Island still had to comply with regulation No. 84 issued way back on 22nd September, 1942. So for a while you could enjoy a sea trip from either Portsmouth or Lymington, but you could not go ashore. However all this changed on 25th August, 1944, the day Paris was liberated by the French 2nd Armoured Division, when all restrictions on travel to and from the Island were lifted for good. Fortunately for the SR the holiday season was almost over, and many people were still hard at work with the War effort as there was still much to be achieved in Europe and elsewhere. Even so there was serious congestion at Portsmouth, so much so that season ticket holders had to be given priority and on occasions severe restrictions had to be placed on the number of tickets issued. The trouble was, of course, that with only two boats available out of the

PS Shanklin leaving Southampton 29th June, 1943

PS *Shanklin* stayed with the SR throughout the War except for a short periods. In December 1941 she was narrowly missed by a destroyer and thrown against Ryde Pier, which resulted in her being out of service for a week whilst her sponson was repaired. The picture shows her starting out for Portsmouth following her annual survey. The journey did not go well as she was in collision with SS *Aid*, a Government stores ship, in misty conditions. The damage to her bows resulted in her having to return to Southampton for repairs.

F. Hawkes

pre-war seven, they could not hope to cater for the sudden increase in business. As far as the SR was concerned the count-down to a resumption of peace-time working began in earnest. Firstly the General Manager asked G.H.R. Gardner, assistant for the Isle of Wight railways, for his suggestions to be considered by the 'Post-War Planning Committee' regarding travel in his area as well as to and from the mainland. He was obviously aware of the facilities which were constructed during World War I between the Royal and Town piers in Southampton docks for train ferries and which, even then, were being extended for use in connection with the invasion of France, so it was not surprising that he put forward the following suggestion in his report:

'A ferry vessel should be designed to carry cars [and] passengers as well as 15 covered rail vans'. No doubt he had in mind a ship similar to the Landing Ship Tank (LST) which was to operate from the aforementioned terminal. This had a single track 'wheeled platform' ramp which was attached to the stern of the ship with points leading to three internal tracks. On the Island the craft was to be run to a point south of Medina Wharf where on waste ground a new terminal could be constructed. With the special tidal characteristics in the area the idea no doubt seemed attractive especially as loading/unloading could have been undertaken in eight out of twelve hours providing the gradient did not exceed 1 in 11. Alas this proposal did not find favour and lapsed.

The five-year building programme was agreed before the end of the year with negotiations starting straight away with William Denny Bros Ltd of Dumbarton for the new vessels required, which would be supplied to the SR under the normal single tender procedure for ships.

The decision had been based on the fact that before the War traffic in the summer had been on the increase and therefore the war-time losses (PS *Portsdown* and PS *Southsea*) should be replaced as soon as possible, particularly bearing in mind that by 1948 PS *Shanklin* would be life-expired. On the other hand the car ferry working out of Portsmouth to Fishbourne did not justify any new craft as there appeared still to be a limited amount of spare capacity. However, it was realised that when finally a decision had to be made to renew this part of the fleet there would be a need to enlarge the terminal facilities at Fishbourne, The arrival of MV *Lymington* on the Lymington-Yarmouth service had transformed the fortunes on this route to the Island. Vehicular traffic was on the increase as well as profitabilty. The PS *Solent* built way back in 1902 was well beyond her life expectancy, having been written off before 1935, and therefore there was a justifiable case to replace her with a specially constructed car ferry vessel.

So in the run up to Nationalisation the SR had taken steps to ensure that for the foreseeable future services to/from the IOW could cater satisfactorily with public requirements and make a return on capital invested.

It was one thing to have defeated the Germans, but the excesses of the weather had still to be endured. On 24th October there was a south-westerly gale, which at times reached 90 mph, accompanied by torrential rain which lasted for several days. These high seas in the Solent caused the cancellation of part of the boat service to Ryde for three days, and on two days there was no car ferry to Fishbourne.

PS Sandown in Portsmouth Harbour July 1939
The layout of the two SR paddle steamers is well demonstrated by this delightful photograph. Behind the *Sandown* is the Gosport car ferry with the word 'Harry Landing'. The Gosport passenger ferry is just visible to the right of the picture.

National Railway Museum

Chapter Two

The Portsmouth-Ryde Service

At the outbreak of war the SR had seven coal-burning paddle steamers on this most popular route to the IOW, which operated between the railway terminals at Portsmouth Harbour and Ryde Pier Head, a distance of about five miles.

Name	Knots	Crew	Passenger Certificate (Winter)
Merstone	13.5	14	723
Portsdown	13.5	14	723
Ryde	14.0	30	1,011
Sandown	14.0	30	974
Shanklin	12.0	19	700
Southsea	16.0	29	1,183
Whippingham	16.0	29	1,183

As can be seen from the above statement, the economics of operation would have varied considerably since doubling the crew did not result in a proportional increase in the number of passengers the boat was permitted to convey. Even for a small boat such as the PS *Portsdown* the spread of duties could be quite appreciable as the following statement shows:

Captain	1	First Engineer	1	Seamen	3
Mate	1	Second Engineer	1	Stewards	2
Purser	1	Firemen	2	Boys	2
				TOTAL	14

The British Navy had long been regarded as the Senior Service which has been merited as a result of forethought and constructive action on the day. This can be illustrated by the fact that the Admiralty agreed with the SR on 1st January, 1937 - over two years before the War - that PS *Portsdown* could be requisitioned at short notice for use within the limits of the Portsmouth Command, but this action may have been in connection with the Navy Review held on 20th May, 1937.

The effect of air raids on civilian population in the Spanish Civil War was not lost on Local Authorities in England. So, when it seemed almost certain that Britain would shortly be at war with Germany, the decision was taken in Portsmouth, following tests on 27th July, 1939, to evacuate all children - some with their parents - to places of safety in the immediate rural areas, having regard to the presence of the naval depot which would be a prime target for enemy aircraft.

Thursday 31st August, 1939 at 14.00 hrs witnessed the last sailing from Ryde Pier to Bournemouth - for 3s. 3d. return. It was not surprising that on the following day there was an almost total lack of business emanating from South Parade Pier, Southsea and as a result the ferries ceased to call there on their way

PS Portsdown

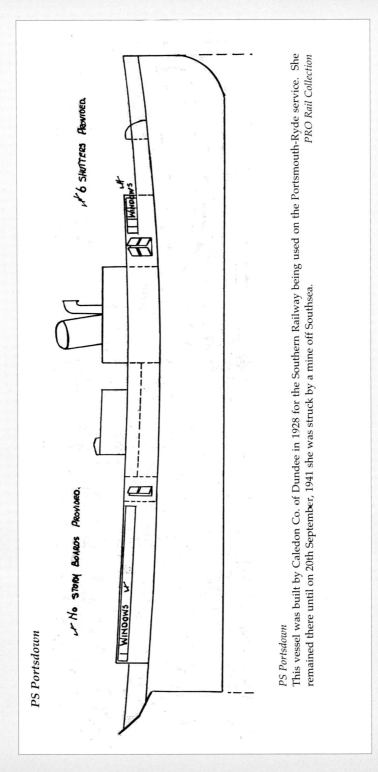

PS Portsdown
This vessel was built by Caledon Co. of Dundee in 1928 for the Southern Railway being used on the Portsmouth-Ryde service. She remained there until on 20th September, 1941 she was struck by a mine off Southsea.

PRO Rail Collection

PS Portsdown

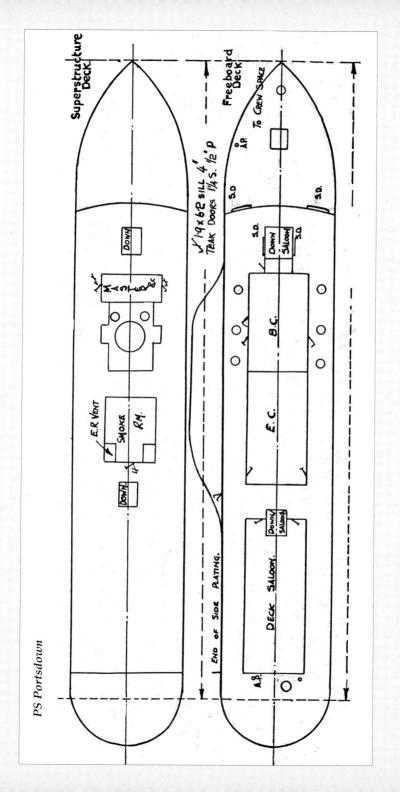

to Ryde, till after the War.

The Authorities had been in touch with the SR regarding arrangements for the evacuation of Portsmouth and had agreed a train and shipping programme, for strange as it may seem the decision had been taken to send about half of the evacuees to the Isle of Wight. This may have seemed rather illogical as there were two prime targets in towns specifically designated to receive them: Cowes with its well-known aircraft factories and shipbuilding yards, and Ventnor with its Radar aircraft location system, both of which were later to be heavily bombed.

The arrangements for travel to the Island were as under:

SECRET

SOUTHERN RAILWAY

| SPECIAL NOTICE |
| EVACUATION No. 2. W |

LONDON WEST AND SOUTHERN DIVISIONS.

SPECIAL TRAIN ARRANGEMENTS
IN CONNECTION WITH
EVACUATION OF PORTSMOUTH,
ISLE OF WIGHT ARRANGEMENTS.

From	To	NUMBER OF REFUGEES.	
		First Day.	Second Day.
Southsea (Clarence Pier)	Ryde	3,242	3,753
	Bembridge	400	330
	Brading	223	—
	Sandown	988	988
	Shanklin	1,000	1,181
	Wroxall	200	290
	Ventnor	1,334	1,024
	Newchurch	214	—
	Haven Street	150	—
	Wootton	—	400
	Newport	1,830	1,767
	Cowes	1,150	1,150
	Calbourne	101	—
	Ningwood	104	—
	Yarmouth	144	—
	Freshwater	860	1,007
	Total	12,000	11,800

The number of refugees sent to each place must not exceed the above totals.

The Boat Service between Southsea, Clarence Pier and Ryde will be :—

NUMBER OF REFUGEES.	CLARENCE PIER Depart.	RYDE PIER Arrive.	RYDE PIER Depart.	CLARENCE PIER Arrive.
	A.M.	A.M.	A.M.	A.M.
900	8 30	9 0	9 15	9 45
1,100	9 0	9 30	9 45	10 15
1,000	9 40	10 10	10 30	11 0
900	10 10	10 40	10 55	11 25
1,100	10 45	11 15	11 30	12 0
			P.M.	P.M.
900	11 45	12 15	12 30	1 0
	P.M.	P.M.		
1,000	12 30	1 0	1 15	1 45
900	1 30	2 0	2 15	2 45
1,000	2 15	2 45	3 0	3 30
1,100	2 45	3 15	3 30	4 0
1,000	3 45	4 15	4 30	5 0
1,100	4 15	4 45	5 0	5 30

From this it would seem that two additional boats would be required, presumably those normally used for excursion working on the 'round-the-Island' trip and to Bournemouth, with some additional sailings found by making adjustments to the normal shipping service.

However, the level of take-up was far less than anticipated, even taking into account the later revision, as the following figures demonstrate

Date	Additional Sailings		Number of Evacuees		
	Proposed	Actual	Proposed	Revision	Actual
1st September, 1939	12	8	12,000	8,600	4,040
2nd September, 1939	12	5	11,800	5,700	1,070
	24	13	23,800	14,300	5,110

The reduced numbers of people on the first day enabled the authorities to use three of the afternoon sailings for the conveyance of 76 patients from Portsmouth General Hospital, of which 40 were stretcher cases. On arrival at Ryde Pier they were transferred by ambulances to four hospitals on the Island.

There matters rested until 24th September, 1939, when under War Regulations PS *Sandown* was requisitioned for conversion to a minesweeper. The alterations were to be undertaken in the SR's Marine Workshops at Southampton Docks, and were to include the provision of a twin Boulton Paul gun turret (designed for use on bombers) and a wireless office. No sooner had this work been carried out than the Ministry stated, on 4th November, that they would like to requisition either PS *Ryde* or PS *Shanklin*. However, the railway when considering their reduced commitments against the cost of working, countered with the suggestion that they take either the PS *Southsea* or PS *Whippingham* instead, as both of these craft had been specially adapted for working outside the comparatively calm waters of the Solent and Spithead. It took time for the Ministry to make a final decision but when it came on 12th February, 1940 the message was that they wanted both PS *Ryde* and PS *Southsea*. They were to be sent to Camper & Nicholson's yard at Northam for adaptation as minesweepers, which involved them being fitted with an 'Oropesa' sweep. These were trailed at the end of the sweep wire which cut the mooring wires of the mine. The latter then rose to the surface and was destroyed by gunfire. The ferries apparently did not reach the yard for two weeks as they had to wait for a suitable high tide to float them up the Itchen river.

So, in the space of six months the SR had managed to hire out nearly half of the Portsmouth-Ryde fleet to the Government, when under normal circumstances they would not have been gainfully employed.

Portsmouth, of course, had its problems owing to the presence of the Navy, but negotiations had ensured that services would not be unreasonably delayed, as the following carefully phrased comment in the Special Traffic Notice of the SR for Christmas 1939 stated:

ISLE OF WIGHT SERVICE

Owing to Navigational and other difficulties passengers for the Isle of Wight are advised to travel from Waterloo, the last service being 12.45 p.m.

The end of the 'Phoney War' culminated in the evacuation of the British Army from Dunkirk, in which three of the fleet were involved - PS *Portsdown*, PS *Sandown* and PS *Whippingham*. (For details of their exploits see *Appendices Two, Three and Four*.) In the early hours of 30th May, 1940 the Admiralty requisitioned PS *Portsdown* and PS *Whippingham* and manned them with naval crews. PS *Portsdown*, still in her pre-war colours, was under the command of Acting Commander K.M. Greig, RN (retired), Pennant No. J20, who also acted as Senior Officer of the Flotilla. He had a dachshund, who became known as 'Bombproof Bella' because, although the ship was bombed repeatedly on every passage, it was never hit, and the ratings ascribed their ship's preservation to their mascot! Nevertheless the ship did incur some damage, which culminated in her having to go to Southampton for repairs. PS *Sandown*, which was already on hire to the Navy and based at Dover as part of the 10th Minesweeping Flotilla, was placed in the charge of Richard R. Church, RNR. Like her companion before, she also had to go to Southampton for minor repairs. PS *Whippingham* made one trip in the charge of Lt Eric Reed, RNR, whose exploit was truly magnificent.

At a meeting chaired by the First Sea Lord on 29th June, 1940 it was decided that, in view of doubts as to whether French sailors on board the 35 ships in Portsmouth Harbour would continue to fight against the Germans, Admiral James should, in the early hours of 3rd July, use his Royal Marines to take over peacefully all the French ships in the Harbour. So that the 3,700 crew members could be away from the area to enable the authorities to question diligently each man about his future intentions, arrangements were made to requisition PS *Shanklin* and PS *Whippingham* to take the Frenchmen up Southampton Water and transfer them to the *Athlone Castle* and *Strathnaven*.

Up to 9th July movement to and from the Isle of Wight was not restricted, but following the advance of the Germans across Northern France the authorities issued an order prohibiting the movement of people by ship for holidays and/or pleasure. Even before this restriction had come into force the effect of the War can be gauged from the undermentioned figures:

Period	Passengers to Isle of Wight (via Ryde)
September 1938 to June 1939	1,339,007
September 1939 to June 1940	767,416
Decrease	571,591 (= 43%)

When PS *Ryde's* conversion was finished she was placed under the command of Lt (later Lt-Cdr) J.C. Allen, Pennant No. J 132, and reached Dover in mid-June, meeting up with PS *Sandown*. The two paddle steamers being well matched for speed (though PS *Ryde* was slightly faster) frequently swept together in the Straits of Dover, which was their happy hunting ground for mines. The German bombers had not yet started their action against the mainland of Britain, but they had found that the mines which they had carefully laid were being swept by these two paddle steamers. In consequence PS *Ryde* and PS *Sandown* became a target for the Luftwaffe and also had the doubtful honour of being mentioned in German radio 'despatches'. 'We shall bomb the *Ryde* and *Sandown* today if they go sweeping' was the sort of threat that came across over the radio. Both ships

HMS Ryde mine-sweeper and coastal flak ship
PS *Ryde* was the last of the paddle steamers to be built for the SR. She was requisitioned in February 1940 by the Navy and following conversion her new duties took her into the Straits of Dover and then into the North Sea. By 1942 new mine-sweepers were available so she was further altered and took up her duties as a decoy for German aircraft off Harwich. Following the cessation of hostilities she was quickly returned to the SR in July 1945 and stayed on station until 1969 when she was withdrawn from service.
Portsmouth Record Office

had several narrow escapes and 'near-misses' which spouted up huge volumes of water and completely hid them from the attacking aircraft. This twice led the Germans into reporting on their return that the *Ryde* and *Sandown* had been sunk.

PS *Sandown's* most remarkable feat of survival was when 22 dive-bombers swooped down upon her during minesweeping operations, dropped over 100 bombs and failed to register a single hit. Shrapnel marks from near misses were the only sign of damage. Another exciting experience was when a near-miss from an exploding mine threw up her stern, sent her bows below water until her forward gun platform was completely submerged, and she see-sawed back until her stern went under and water flooded the engine room to a depth of two feet. Eventually the Admiralty decided that they would be better employed elsewhere, so in September they moved off together into the North Sea to Granton, where they formed part of the 7th Minesweeping Flotilla under the Rosyth Command.

PS *Southsea*, when she emerged from Camper & Nicholson's yard fitted with minesweeping equipment, had also been armed with a 4 inch breech-loading quick-fire (BLQF) gun, a set of twin half-inch guns of Vickers origin in a turret, plus two Lewis guns and a Holman Projector. The Holman Projector was one of those strange anti-aircraft (AA) inventions which was adopted by the Navy. In essence it consisted of a 2 ft-long tube about nine inches in diameter fixed towards the stern of the deck at an angle of about 60 degrees facing upwards and overboard. The charge resembled a rocket which, when it exploded, ejected a parachute which had trailing from it a thin wire in the hope that this would get entangled with the propellor(s) of the enemy aircraft. It seems to

Holman Projector as used on PS Sandown by the Navy
This rocket apparatus was developed in the early days of the war and fired a rocket to which was attached a parachute with long wires dangling. The idea was that this would get entangled with enemy aircraft swooping to attack the ship. In reality these weapons were hated by ships crews as the rocket wires invariably got tangled in the ship's rigging.
The Trustees of the Imperial War Museum

have been more of a morale booster than an efficient AA weapon as there is no record of this gun ever being successful. The Navy commissioned the ship on 2nd July and, following coaling, a test run was undertaken over a measured mile, which showed she was capable of sustaining a speed of 13.67 knots.

At the end of her first 10 days under Naval command she came into contact with HMS *Ailsey*, a minesweeping trawler, which caused slight damage to her offside. Eventually she left the Southampton area flying Pennant J 133 to take up her duties with the 8th Minesweeping Flotilla under the Rosyth Command at North Shields, at 06.40 on 23rd July. She put into Dover at 15.45 for coaling etc. and left again at 04.45 on 25th July, arriving at her destination the next morning at 08.30. The 28th July saw her on her first minesweeping duty, but nemesis was soon at hand for on 3rd August, at 14.05 she was in collision with the tug *Great Emperor*, which resulted in slight damage to her plating. Eight days later another collision took place, this time with the *Luguna Belle*, which affected her off-side sponson. After these minor incidents it is not surprising to learn that on 28th August the Naval authorities put her into Albert Edward dock for repairs. Whilst she was there the opportunity was taken to increase her fire-power by exchanging the 4-inch BLQF for a 12-pounder gun. When she emerged she joined the 7th Minesweeping Flotilla instead, which was also based at North Shields.

The PS *Southsea* was soon in the news for on 17th October her Naval crew under the command of Lt C.C.M. Pawley, RNR shot down a Dornier 17, and in grateful recognition of the crew's splendid effort the General Manager of the SR sent a cheque for £10 to be used for the benefit of the crew. This was used to purchase two armchairs for the ward room. Alas the PS *Southsea's* life was soon to be cut short for on 16th February whilst minesweeping off the Tyne, she was herself mined. With great effort she did manage to reach the shore and be beached, but on inspection was considered to be a constructive loss. The railway, however, did get their annual hire charge of £6,218 and after the war 25 per cent of her basic value when the replacement MV *Southsea* arrived from Denny's of Dumbarton.

Meanwhile, back at Portsmouth the situation had changed, for on 12th August, 1940 Portsmouth Harbour station had its first taste of what was to come in the way of bombing. The repeat came in the early hours of 7th October when one of the bombs fell into the mud and damaged the north corner of the pier. Whilst repairs were being quickly put in hand, the 09.30 boat from Ryde and the return working at 11.30 were diverted to Clarence Pier, which had been specially reopened following consultation with the military authorities, who had closed it down from 4th July.

Southampton docks were severely blitzed during the night of 30th November/1st December when the water mains were put out of action. To help the Docks in their hour of need one of the Portsmouth-Ryde fleet was despatched to Southampton with fire appliances which resulted in it being back too late to work the 07.25 service from Portsmouth to the Isle of Wight.

Portsmouth will always remember the night of 10th/11th January, 1941 when the Germans dropped over 25,000 bombs on the city to devastating effect, which included the destruction of the city's electricity works. The first raid started at 18.03 and lasted until 22.25. Luckily the ships' staff managed to put out all the incendiaries despite the fact that a test at 21.00 proved that an HE bomb had cut off the water supplies. The second raid, which started at 22.38 and lasted till 02.10, was

Bomb damaged PS Whippingham at Southampton 24th January, 1941
PS *Whippingham* was one of the largest paddle steamers owned by the SR for the Portsmouth-Ryde route. She was requisitioned to help with the evacuation of Dunkirk, carrying over 2,700 on one trip. Later she carried French sailors from Portsmouth to Southampton for interrogation. Whilst she was at Southampton for general overhaul she was bombed and requisitioned by the Navy. Following a spell as a mine-sweeper and an AA ship she eventually returned to her peacetime role in May 1946. It was 1963 before she was eventually scrapped.

National Maritime Museum

PS Merstone near Ryde Pier 5th July, 1943
PS *Merstone* was one of the smaller paddle steamers which the SR had during the War to operate Portsmouth-Ryde service. She is shown loaded with troops and a sprinkling of civilians. As the passengers crowd towards the starboard side of the ship, preparatory to disembarking at Ryde, the vessel takes a list, with the result that the waters thrown up by the paddle wheels pour out of the paddle box.

F. Hawkes

of a much more serious nature. Although two members of the ship's crew had been allowed home because their houses had been bombed, the crew of the night mail PS *Merstone* moored alongside the harbour jetty used the ship's fire-fighting hoses to extinguish the fires in the general offices and the Marine Manager's office on the station. In addition, the jetty had received a direct hit which severely damaged the concrete decking and associated steelwork. The resultant damage necessitated an instruction being given at 08.05 to Ryde to hold the ferry for Portsmouth until the jetty was made safe. Eventually at 13.20 permission was granted for it to proceed to Portsmouth. The lack of electricity at Portsmouth meant that the ferries could only sail during daylight hours for the next two days and during this period the milk traffic from the IOW was conveyed on the Fishbourne car ferry.

A few weeks later the PS *Merstone* was unlucky, as on the morning of 23rd January, 1941, whilst proceeding slowly into Portsmouth Harbour during thick fog, she collided with a Government trawler. PS *Merstone* sustained £200 worth of damage to her bows, which the SR considered should be paid for by the Government as the trawler was thought not to have been proceeding in the appropriate fashion. PS *Merstone* was soon in the news again, for the evening of 9th March brought further raids to Portsmouth. At 22.00 hrs incendiaries rained down on the paddle steamers whilst they were tied up alongside the jetty and once again the staff took the appropriate action by putting them over the side. Unfortunately fitter R.O. Davies on the *Merstone*, who was carrying out repairs, sustained burns to his face and legs and had to be taken to hospital. The same happened on the adjacent PS *Sandown* where deck hand F.W. Cottrell received damage to his eyes, and to complete the trio of injuries 2nd Engineer E.G. Leggett on the PS *Portsdown* suffered bomb shock. It is pleasing to mention however that records show all three men were back at work within six months. Meanwhile a high-explosive bomb had fallen into the water at the south end of the jetty which damaged some of the piles as well as PS *Portsdown*. This necessitated the 04.00 sailing having to be cancelled and another boat having to be got ready to cover the 06.35 sailing which left at 07.30. The damage to PS *Portsdown* was soon rectified and the ferry resumed her normal working with the 13.30 sailing.

During the evening of 24th May a lone Junkers JU88 appeared over the Island and attempted to bomb the Cement Mills on the River Medina, but the bombs missed their target and instead fell adjacent to the single track railway between Newport and Cowes, the blasting derailed the 19.12 train from Newport consisting of two coaches. The pilot then flew around looking for a suitable target for the rest of his bombs and espied PS *Shanklin* working the 19.45 service from Portsmouth to Ryde. The bomber lined up on its target and dropped its load from about 200 ft but missed the ship, no doubt owing to the Captain's presence of mind to alter course at the critical moment. Not content, it made another run and machine-gunned it, but fortunately no casualties or damage were sustained. In the summer PS *Whippingham* was put into the Marine Workshops at Southampton for attention and whilst there the Admiralty decided on 8th September to requisition her for conversion to a minesweeper (J136). The conversion was destined to be sadly delayed, for during the night of 30th November/1st December she received a direct hit to her paddle box causing extensive damage to her superstructure.

PORTSMOUTH CATHEDRAL

Order of Service

In Memory of Passengers and
Crew of Southern Railway
Steamer who lost their lives on
Saturday, 20th September, 1941

———

19TH OCTOBER, 1941

THE UNDERMENTIONED MEMBERS OF THE
SHIP'S CREW LOST THEIR LIVES:

CAPTAIN H. A. CHANDLER

MATE S. S. BURGESS

PURSER E. H. COTTRELL

FIREMAN W. HARRISON

FIREMAN B. RAWLINS

SEAMAN A. J. FAREY

SEAMAN J. MONK

ORDINARY SEAMAN E. BURNETT

It was not uncommon for German aircraft to lay mines during the hours of darkness in the approaches to Portsmouth Harbour. The Admiralty therefore made continuous efforts to ensure that all navigational channels were frequently swept by minesweepers. So the event of Saturday 20th September, 1941 came as more than a great shock to all those involved. For years the SR had been under obligation to the Post Office to provide a night time sailing from Portsmouth to Ryde for the conveyance of mails intended for early morning delivery. On this day the 04.00 service was worked by PS *Portsdown* and was in the Swashway, a small channel through the Hamilton Bank near Spitsand Fort. The Navy had good reason to remember this bank for it was here in the 1930s that the battleship HMS *Nelson* ran aground and was only released when her crew were sent forward and told to jump in unison to help the tugs.

At this point in the journey it was the custom to empty the ashes from the furnaces overboard after leaving harbour, so most of the crew would have been just forward of the paddle box to carry out this operation. It was almost dead low water, and they were in a position where Captain Chandler would have ordered an increase in speed. There was an enormous explosion which tore the vessel in half, just forward of amidships where most of the officers and crew would have been at that time, killing eight of the crew of eleven, including the Senior Captain, Mr H.A. Chandler, his Mate, Mr S. Burgess, 12 out of the 29 service passengers and three out of eight civilian passengers.

Sam Jupe, a young deckhand who was bow lookout, had a miraculous escape. Although injured and not a strong swimmer, he managed to dive over the side and, holding on to a piece of wreckage, swam to the stern where he climbed aboard. The bow section meantime had swung right round and turned turtle.

The stern sank but stayed on an even keel, with part of the deck above water. Mr W.H. Kreutzer, the Chief Engineer and Mr H.J.O. Allen, the Second Engineer, had been further aft, which saved their lives. Although injured and badly shocked the three survivors managed to launch the two lifeboats, saving many of the passengers.

On board that night had been Captain William Gibson who was due to relieve Captain Chandler at 06.00 hours. It was quite usual to sleep aboard in order to avoid the difficulties of early morning transport to the Harbour Station.

Gibson had attended a function that night and was unable to get home to Portchester, so decided to come on board and snatch a few hours sleep in the after smoking cabin. By going to this cabin spared his life, for no doubt, had he gone to one of the duty officers' cabins he would certainly have perished; so he became a survivor.*

Searchlights were played on the scene and small Naval boats were sent out to rescue the survivors, who were taken either to Haslar Hospital or to the Harbour Pier. Second Engineer Allen and Sam Jupe were taken to Haslar, but were soon released, although it was to be some months before the former fully recovered. The First Engineer was uninjured, but was suffering slightly from shock. Early in the morning the Mate's twin brother, George Burgess, was cycling to the Harbour for the start of his duty, when a signalman called from his box that one of the steamers had been sunk. He hurried to the harbour

---

* Extract from Miss Sherwood's unpublished MS entitled 'The House at the Point'.

station to discover that Seth, aged 33 years, had been lost.

For a list of the crew who perished in this sad event *see page 26*. Mr Pelly, Divisional Marine Manager, obtained the use of a Naval pinnace and by 06.00 went out to the wreck. With Mr Traill, the First Engineer and two deckhands, they searched for survivors or bodies, but found neither. The bodies of the crew were never found, and at a later date a memorial service was held in Portsmouth Cathedral. In cold hard financial terms at the time of her sinking her depreciated value was £15,918, but her replacement would cost in the order of £55,000. The SR management opened a fund for the 'next of kin' which by 14th January, 1942 had reached £382. In addition the SR paid £2 10s. per week for the first 10 weeks to the widows. Two of them decided to leave Portsmouth, Mrs Cottrell going to Ryde and Mrs Harrison to Uxbridge. In both cases the SR paid the entire cost of the move. The wreck remained visible at low tide until removed by the Admiralty in 1945.

The Naval authorities had always been very concerned about the authorised routes into Portsmouth Harbour lest a German U-boat take advantage of this and follow a boat into the harbour and it was not surprising that this matter came to a head in October 1941. The Admiralty on this date issued an order changing the route from that with four unlighted buoys to one of 16 buoys on a channel with varying widths. The SR stated that this was too dangerous for paddle steamers and therefore the service would have to be suspended after dark. However, to give the Admiralty time to have second thoughts on the matter, they said the boats would continue to operate in the dark, subject to the discretion of the ship's captain. They pointed out that if the order was put into effect the 19.25 sailing (*see (a) on timetable below*) from Ryde which carried all the outwards mail would have to be cancelled, similarly the cancellation of the 04.00 sailing from Portsmouth (*see timetable*) would seriously retard the deliveries on the Island. In addition, having services restricted to daylight hours would affect the availability of workers from the Island who were employed in the Dockyard. It was not surprising therefore that a meeting was convened on 13th October between the SR, the Post Office and the Admiralty to try to find an amicable solution. Eventually on 23rd December the Admiralty compromised by permitting four of the buoys to be illuminated.

Though the service as given below was still quite substantial, civilian use was only about 20 per cent owing to travel restrictions, the remainder being members of the armed forces, both military and naval. From a census taken over 18 days in July 1941 about 24,000 persons were conveyed on this route, though in a similar period in November this had reduced to about 17,500. For full details see *Appendix Six*.

Portsmouth-Ryde Boat Service, October 1941

Weekdays

		(a)	(b)						(a)
Portsmouth Hbr	*dep.*	0400	0635	0830	1100	1300	1445	1700	1855
Ryde Pier	*arr.*	0435	0710	0905	1135	1335	1520	1735	1925
Ryde Pier	*dep.*	0500*	0735	0930	1200	1435	1635	1740	1925
Portsmouth Hbr	*arr.*	0535*	0810	1005	1235	1510	1710	1815	2005

		Sundays					
		(b)					(a)
Portsmouth Hbr	dep.	0725	1000	1155	1450	1630	1905
Ryde Pier	arr.	0800	1035	1230	1525	1705	1935
Ryde Pier	dep.	0835	1055	1310	1535	1725	1935
Portsmouth Hbr	arr.	0930	1130	1345	1610	1800	2010

Notes: (a) Trips to be cancelled in winter months
        (b) Trips which may be cancelled awaiting daylight
       * = Empty working

Naval craft were always dashing hither and thither in the area and on 11th December one came too close to PS *Shanklin* and threw her hard against the pier at Ryde. The starboard sponson sustained £299 worth of damage, which necessitated her being out of use for six days. During this period the SR hired PS *Princess Helena* from the Red Funnel Line at a cost of £104 5s. PS *Shanklin's* troubles were not over for, a little while afterwards, when proceeding back to Portsmouth after completion of a survey at Southampton, she was in collision with SS *Aid* a Government stores ship, with resultant damage estimated at £750. Apparently the weather at the time was misty and reports indicated that the SS *Aid* was on the wrong side of the channel and failing to sound her foghorn at the proper interval.

As mentioned earlier, the paddle steamers were bunkered from a coal hulk moored in Portsmouth Harbour. Whether it was the result of constant wash from passing naval craft or just age we shall never know, but suddenly in December it was found essential to renew the (1935) mooring ropes with new ones, which were supplied by the Admiralty at a cost of £800.

The year 1942 saw another scheme promoted by the Admiralty, which nearly resulted in the cessation of the service to Ryde. Back in 1935 the first Motor Torpedo Boats arrived at the shore based establishment known as HMS *Vernon* situated in the Gun Wharf at Portsmouth. This site suffered greatly from the air raids in December 1940 and March 1941, which resulted in some of the Naval activities being transferred to Loch Long, Weston-super-Mare and Roedean girls school! However, by November 1942 the Admiralty deemed it safe enough to warrant returning some of these activities. Planning for 'D' day was now under formulation and one aspect involved the provision of adequate mooring and repair facilities for their Coastal Forces Unit to be known as Force 'S'. The initial idea was transmitted to the local SR management on 17th November. The accompanying plan envisaged the small jetty being replaced by three set at an angle of 60 degrees to the shore line and extending out for 240 ft, i.e. 50 ft in front of the line from the railway pontoon. This was over an area earmarked by the local authority for post-war redevelopment. The SR's local Docks and Marine management took great exception to this scheme, but two meetings at local level proved abortive. So the SR elevated the matter to the Railway Executive, which on 15th May, 1943 followed this up with the Minister of Transport personally. The C-in-C at Portsmouth for his part stated that in his opinion the SR's objections could be summarised as follows:

(a) The difficulty in maintaining their normal passenger and mail services to and from
     the Isle of Wight in all weathers and at all states of the tide if the approach to the
     railway pontoon fpom the south is obstructed in any way.
(b) Doubt as to the Admiralty's post-war policy. SR will not acquiesce willingly in any
     scheme which, if permanent, would interfere with their own policy of expansion
     after the war.
(c) Possible interferences with free access to the mud berths to the north side of the
     War Department wharf, which the SR use when overhauling their steamers.

A meeting was convened at the Ministry on 4th June at which the SR were
represented by Captain Pelly the Divisional Marine Manager and his assistant,
Captain Jefferies. To the Admiralty's horror the Chairman of the meeting turned
out to be R.P. Biddle (former SR Chairman of their Shipping Fleet) who had been
seconded to the Ministry to head their shipping department. The matter was
ventilated and one interesting fact to emerge was that the coaling stage was only
used by the SR every other day. The Admiralty acquiesced and eventually on
17th June produced alternative plans which were acceptable to the SR, and at the
same time agreed to draw up Navigational Orders for craft using the new jetties
to the effect that they must not hamper the SR ship movements. The Treasury
agreed to the altered scheme, costing £59,000, on 8th July.

With the arrival of more purpose-built minesweepers on the North Sea coast
the PS *Ryde* and PS *Sandown* became redundant, so in March 1942 they were
transferred to shipyards on the Thames for fitting out as 'Eagle' ships. In reality
these were coastal flak ships which operated independently with a view to
shooting down the unwary member of the Luftwaffe who thought they were an
easy target.

Ryde's armament consisted of:

Starboard

		Boulton-Paul 4x .303 Power-operated Gun Turret		
	OERLIKON		OERLIKON	POMPOM
Bow POMPOM	(SEARCH		(Twin Rocket	
	(LIGHT	Boulton-Paul	(Lewis Gun	**Stern**
	OERLIKON	4x.303 Power-operated Gun Turret	OERLIKON	POMPOM

Port

After conversion PS *Ryde* was sent to Sheerness and PS *Sandown* was allocated to
Nore Command, Humber area, being based initially at Grimsby and afterwards
at Immingham. Eventually towards the end of 1943 she moved to Harwich.

As the war progressed the availability of labour became more and more
difficult as each schedule of Reserved Occupations was issued. Indeed, by the
summer of 1943 the Manager at Portsmouth was hinting that, even if there was
only a small amount of sickness during the coming winter, it would be
necessary to reduce the service to one-boat working. On the other hand, the
officials responsible for administering the Reserved Occupation schedules
could make life difficult too, a case in point being that of coalman Howard who

had the unenviable task of filling coal sacks on the coal hulk as part of the operation for bunkering the paddle steamers. Apparently the officials considered that this work was not covered by the list of Reserved Occupations so proposed to withdraw him from the shipping service. Great protestations took place and eventually an amicable solution was found.

The 'D' Day preparations at Portsmouth for the invasion of France may have cast doubt on the continued availability of the service from Portsmouth to Ryde in 1943, and in the event the actual operation itself did require its closure, fortunately for only a limited period. In April 1944 the Director of Sea Transport, Ministry of War Transport advised the Railway Executive that the two remaining paddle steamers working the Portsmouth Ryde route would be required for special duties which could last as long as seven days. Initially the SR was advised that the Red Funnel line was to provide *Princess* and *Solent Queen* for the service, with landing at the Portsmouth end being made via the South Parade Pier, but examination of this structure showed that it was not safe enough for use by civilians, so the scheme was dropped. Thus it was reluctantly agreed that there would be a temporary closure of the service, resulting in all passengers being redirected onto the car ferry working from Broad Street to Fishbourne, with bus connections laid on to Ryde.

Following the attack during the night of 25th/26th April 1944 by Dornier 217s and Junkers JU88s of KG 166, the Admiralty suspended the movement of all boats within Portsmouth Harbour for eight hours because of the suspected presence of a mine. SR ships sustained no damage during this attack or the one on the following night, which marked the end of air raids on Portsmouth.

One of the problems which the Admiralty encountered when planning the loading arrangements in connection with 'D' Day was the fact that there were insufficient berths for all the ships involved. One of the ways used to overcome this problem was to anchor some of the ships out in the Solent and use the SR paddle steamers to ferry out the men together with their equipment from Portsmouth.

The Military, who now had the necessary dispensation regarding emergency arrangements for travel to and from the Island, issued orders on 28th April to the effect that the service would be withdrawn between 05.00 on 1st May and 00.01 on 3rd May. This effectively ensured that on only one day was the servicing of mails and newspapers affected. However the SR experienced difficulty in explaining to the public how it was that the first service to the Island was not cancelled. Therefore, when the remaining paddle steamers were withdrawn in order to transfer over 4,000 men from the mainland to the ships on 3rd June, even the 04.00 sailing was cancelled. The SR paddle steamers also made a trip to the 'prefabricated' Port of Arromanches (Mulberry harbour) before resuming their normal civilian working.

The three paddle steamers under naval control acted as auxiliary AA ships and served the nation well. PS *Sandown* came from Weymouth to join the Western Task Force and became the 'A' Control vessel at Mulberry harbour on 11th June. Later on in the gale which caused much havoc in the area of Omaha beach on 20th June, she lost her anchor and had to be taken in tow by the tug *Cormorant*. PS *Ryde* on the other hand, fulfilled her task without problems, leaving the Solent on 6th June. Her stay at Omaha lasted from 15th to 21st June

PS Whippingham 15th August, 1954
This was the largest of the Southern Railway paddle steamers having a certificate to convey 1,183 passengers which was greatly exceeded when she conveyed 2,7000 soldiers on one trip from Dunkirk. She was used by the Admiralty to convey French sailors who had been taken off their Warships, from Portsmouth to Southampton in 1940. *B. Moody*

PS Sandown at Newhaven October 1958
Whilst items of maintenance which do not require dry docking were normally carried out at Portsmouth, those which necessitated attention to the hull could only be done at Southampton or Newhaven. *Author's Collection*

before she returnd to England. PS *Whippingham* performed a similar function with the Eastern Task Force following repairs at Southampton in April.

The SR viewed the coming end of hostilities with very mixed feelings. On the one hand the rail services to Portsmouth Harbour should be able to operate satisfactorily as the Board of Trade had agreed to the expenditure of £37,250 to repair the bomb damage at the station. On the other side of the water the Island's railway was virtually ready to reinstate the pre-war train service. The reinforced concrete landing stage made by Christiane & Nielsen for £11,752 in 1931 at Portsmouth had been repaired at a cost of £5,341, which now enabled two vessels to be berthed simultaneously. Two paddle steamers (PS *Merstone* and PS *Shanklin*) were available to work the service and PS *Solent* had been transferred from the Lymington-Yarmouth route to act as relief when either of the other paddle steamers was out of service. In addition, the Admiralty had been prevailed upon to release PS *Ryde* and she was now at Southampton undergoing austerity reconditioning for civilian work.

On the face of it, therefore, the SR would be able to cater satisfactorily for the peacetime conditions, which could mean levels of business above those experienced before the War, even though petrol for cars was still likely to be severely rationed and travel overseas would barely be possible owing to financial constraints, as well as travel problems within Europe. PS *Ryde* duly returned and took up her pre-war working on 7th July, 1945 only to find that one of her capstans needed replacement, so she did not sail again till Friday 13th July.

The return of men from the Forces had hardly got underway so it was not surprising that the SR experienced considerable difficulty in crewing their ships, even though efforts were made at a high level to obtain additional men. In essence only six complete crews were available, which resulted in the following situation:

(a) On Mondays to Fridays the third ship could only be run on one shift.
(b) The fourth ship could not be used on Saturdays as the crew were already working overtime to perform double shifts with three vessels.
(c) On Sundays it was only possible to run two vessels on double shifts.

Passengers' Luggage in Advance created special problems at weekends as in excess of 800 items in cages needed to be moved to and from the Island. So arrangements were made with Messrs Pickfords to charter one of their barges which normally plied between Portsmouth and Cowes with SR freight. Initially the service was as under, but it seems that it only operated for a very limited period:

Saturday	Portsmouth Harbour	*arr.*	06.45	in berth
		dep.	07.15	
	Ryde Pier Head	*arr.*	08.15	
Sunday	Ryde Pier Head	*dep.*	13.00	
	Portsmouth Harbour	*arr.*	14.00	

The increase in traffic showed up another problem. It seems that the gangways had been destroyed in the bombing, so whilst the War continued improvisation was the order of the day. In July it was therefore decided that the

SR coal hulk - C11 - in Portsmouth Harbour with motor boat Alice 8th March, 1963

As the SR had no coal wharf at Portsmouth under its jurisdiction all paddle steamers had to be coaled from this loading barge which was moored off the pontoon by the Harbour station. About once a fortnight she was towed into the naval dockyard where the SR had a rail-connected jetty. Towards the end of 1945 the coal hulk had to be taken away to Southampton for major repairs, which took over two months. In the intervening period the Admiralty renewed the mooring lines and the paddle steamers were bunkered by Fraser & White. *Portsmouth Record Office*

Marine Engineer would produce five new gangways of 16 ft 6 in. in length, but as these were to be manhandled due regard had to be given to their weight. After the Bank Holiday, which then took place on the first Monday in August, the pressure on the shipping front eased and queues which sometimes stretched right back to the Esplanade station at Ryde (!) now returned to more normal proportions. This being so, the decision was taken to defer the recruitment of one First Engineer and three Mates until the spring of the following year. Another factor to be taken into account was the taking of annual leave by shipping staff during the high season. This had been made worse by the fact that the holiday period for wages grades had been doubled from the pre-war quota of six days to twelve days. Management eventually reached a decision with the appropriate Trade Unions to the effect that the taking of annual leave was to be barred during the following periods: two weeks at Easter, one week at Whitsun and from the second week in July till the end of August.

With the approach of Christmas things began to look difficult as PS *Merstone* was away on annual survey, and had been replaced by PS *Freshwater* which had only been returned to the SR on 8th December. PS *Shanklin* was holding the line whilst PS *Ryde* was in the local marine workshops for repairs to her engine and sponson. As things turned out, the Marine Engineer was able to complete the work on PS *Ryde* in time for her to be the third vessel in the working to deal with the Christmas rush, as from 20th December. PS *Whippingham* was still away and even when she was eventually released on 2nd March, 1946, reconditioning had to be carried out and in consequence she did not take up her peacetime role until 15th May, 1946.

So the SR's arrangements for the Portsmouth-Ryde working gave the impression that the future was secure and that a satisfactory return on capital enployed could be reasonably expected. The following steamboat receipts would, on the face of it, show management's judgement to be vindicated:

	Passengers £	Parcels £	Mails £	Misc. £	Total £
1944	47,189	7,429	5,608	17,809	78,034
1945	89,413	6,434	5,619	16,265	117,731
	+42,244	-995	+11	-1,543	+39,697

The level of business eventually achieved, when compared with the pre-war level of passengers, shows only a marginal increase. Unfortunately, this increase could not be maintained when petrol rationing ceased and financial restrictions on foreign travel were lifted.

Year	Passengers to Ryde
1938	1,191,364
1946	1,304,856
1947	1,373,883

MV Fishbourne leaving Portsmouth Harbour

MV *Fishbourne* was the first car ferry constructed for the Fishbourne route in 1927. She is shown here passing Fort Blockhouse (HMS *Dolphin*) with a full load of vehicles. In May 1940 she was requisitioned in connection with the evacuation of the BEF from Dunkirk, but unfortunately her size was against her and she eventually returned without giving any assistance. She normally covered the Fishbourne route throughout the War and continued to do so in peacetime until 1961.

World Ship Society

Chapter Three

The Portsmouth-Fishbourne Service

This car ferry route, which had its first purpose-built diesel-driven vessel in 1927, with another two shortly afterwards, can be considered one of the slowest routes, speed of movement at best being only 8 mph (i.e., double the normal walking pace) so it is not surprising that the journey took 55 minutes. There were other shortcomings which only became apparent as the War progressed.

The military from time to time made use of this route and when the vessel was for their sole use the loading could be as under:

(a) 100 soldiers with three cars and five 3-ton lorries
(b) 100 soldiers with four cars and seven 30-cwt lorries
(c) 100 soldiers with four cars and nine 15-cwt lorries
(d) 100 soldiers with 10 Bren Gun carriers
(e) 600 soldiers without any vehicles

The military obviously had considerable regard for the seamanship of the captains, who managed these small ships in what could be very crowded waters, since with only two lifeboats they would have had to rely on other ships in the area in the unlikely event of the ferry boat sinking.

Generally speaking, except when military requirements dictated otherwise, the service below could be operated by one vessel during daylight hours, except on Tuesdays:

Portsmouth - Camber dock	*dep.*	09.15	*11.45	14.15
Fishbourne - Wootton	*arr.*	10.10	12.40	15.10
Fishbourne - Wootton	*dep.*	11.25	13.55	16.25
Portsmouth - Camber dock	*arr.*	12.20	14.50	17.20

* operated on Tuesdays only

It was not therefore surprising that when the call came in May 1940 for boats to make their way to Dunkirk to rescue the British Expeditionary Force both *Wootton* and *Fishbourne* were released to help in this endeavour, leaving *Hilsea* to cover the service to the Isle of Wight.

Fishbourne gradually made her way up Channel and eventually reached Ramsgate. From here she sailed at 09.20 on 1st June in the tow of two tugs *Duke* and *Princess*. After two hours the *Princess's* towrope suddenly parted and after a little delay a new one was connected. The *Fishbourne's* problems were not over, for at about 12.50 the *Duke* was detached urgently to help tug *Sun III* when the ship was two miles off Dunkirk. Eventually at about 17.35 she joined up with the *Medway Queen* whose Captain, after watching how the small ferry vessel behaved in the Channel waters, decided at 21.12 to signal the Vice-Admiral at Dover suggesting that in view of the circumstances it would be wise for her to return to Ramsgate. This was agreed and she arrived back there at 07.30 in the tow of the *Princess*. Little seems to be known about the activities of the *Wootton* other than the following extract from *1940 - The World in Flames*:

MV Wootton

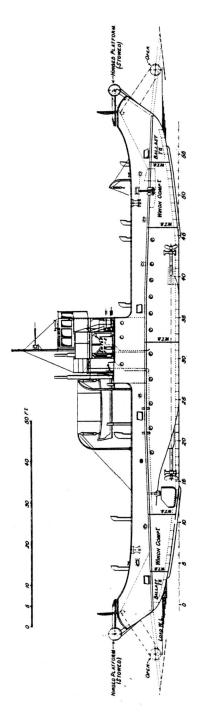

Layout of MV Wootton

MV *Wootton* was constructed in 1928 for the Portsmouth-Fishbourne car ferry route. In May 1940 she was requisitioned and made her way towards Dunkirk, but appears to have taken no active part in the evacuation. Thereafter she spent most of her time as a relief vessel for both the Fishbourne and Lymington routes. The army paid for her link-span to be strengthened in 1942 to permit the carrying of heavy vehicles. It was not until 1961 that she was taken out of service.

A. Brown

MV Wootton

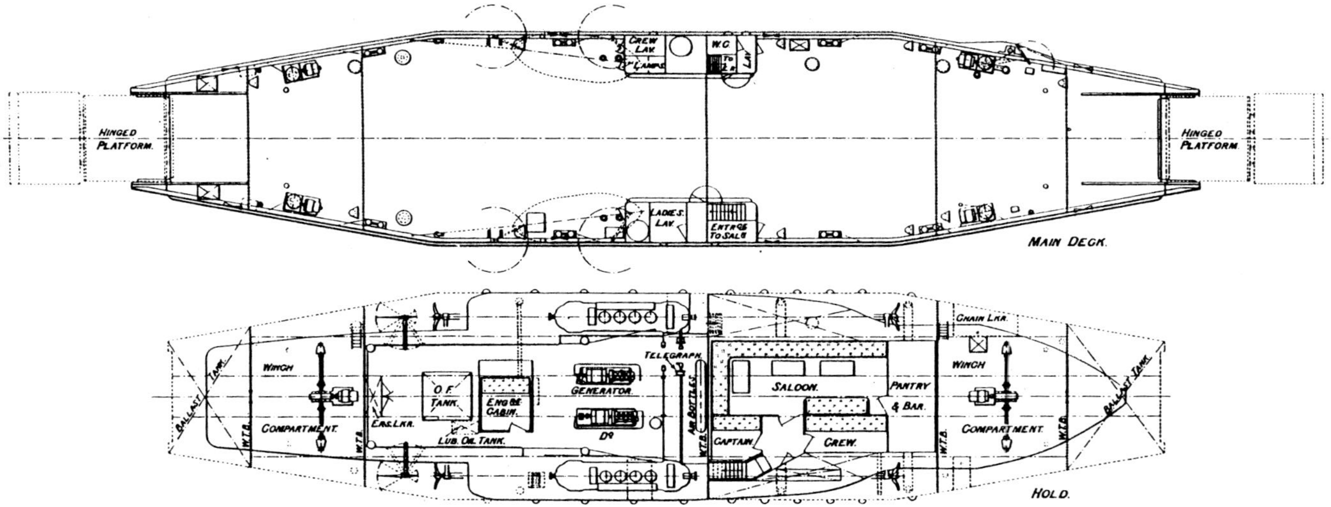

HINGED PLATFORM

MAIN DECK

W.C.

CREW LAV.

LADIES LAV.

LADIES TOILET

HINGED PLATFORM

CHAIN LKR

WINCH

COMPARTMENT

HOLD

PANTRY

& BAR

SALOON

CREW

CAPTAIN

AIR BOTTLES

TELEGRAPH

GENERATOR

DY

ENGINE CABIN

O. TANK

LUB. OIL TANK

ENGINE

W.T.B.

WINCH

COMPARTMENT

MV Hilsea at Fishbourne, Isle of Wight
The rural nature of the slipway by Fishbourne at the entrance to Wootton Creek, some 5½ miles from the centre of Newport, is all too apparent.   *C. Grasemann*

Wootton Creek 1940
This photograph was taken by a member of the German Abwehr organisation for inclusion in a booklet for German soldiers to familiarise them with the Isle of Wight landscape (*see also photograph on page 54*).   *Alderney Museum*

On the bridge of the destroyer HMS *Malcolm*, Lieutenant Ian Cox was moved almost to tears to see the boats led by the *Wootton*, the Isle of Wight car ferry, wallowing like a sawn-off landing stage through the water. His voice shaking with emotion, Cox burst out with the classic lines from Shakespere's *Henry V*, which spoke of another battle in France:

'All gentlemen in England, now abed,
shall think themseves accurs'd they were not here:
And hold their manhoods cheap, while any speaks
that fought with us upon St Crispin's Day.'

So, whilst one can applaud the great efforts that the Naval staff made, it is sad to reflect that the results did not match the endeavours, but they had tried.

Following the fall of France and the evacuation of the Channel Islands, the SR, as mentioned earlier, still operated services to the Isle of Wight. With *Hilsea* normally covering the car-ferrying working to Fishbourne, passengers until May 1941 would have seen alongside the Outer Camber Quay the SR's *Autocarrier*. She was there to have repairs done by the Marine Department as these did not require dry-docking. No doubt they had been caused by her exploits at Dunkirk and earlier at Calais when Capt. C.H. Masters brought back to Folkestone secret military stores which the local dockers refused to unload.

The differences between the two types of car-carrier are as under:

	Hilsea	*Autocarrier*
Built	1930	1931
Gross tonnage	149	822
Net tonnage	70	329
Speed (knots)	8	15
Fuel	Diesel	Coal
Length	121 ft	230 ft
Breadth	26 ft 1 in.	35 ft 8 in.
Depth	7 ft 7 in.	15 ft
Passengers	92	104
Crew	6	20
Cars	18	35
Loading system	ro-ro	crane

The impact of the War on the carryings on this route, before the clampdown on travel to the Island as from 10th July, 1940, can easily be gauged from the undermentioned figures:

	Motor Cars		*Lorries*	
September 1938 - June 1939	12,793		1,833	
September 1939 - June 1940	4,347		1,365	
	- 8,446	(-66%)	-468	(-25%)

So it was not surprising that *Wootton* after her return from Dunkirk was usually at Lymington to assist the operations there as and when necessary.

In the summer of 1941, owing to silting, captains began to experience difficulty at Fishbourne in berthing their vessels at certain states of the tide. It was wartime and the service had a certain benefit to the Government and so it

MV Hilsea in Portsmouth Harbour

MV *Hilsea* is seen leaving the slipway in Portsmouth Harbour just before the War with the Gosport ferry and Camper Nicholson's boat yard in the distance. Although capable of carrying 18 cars, she is shown here with a mixture of trailers, cars and a Church Army van. The two lifeboats were considered sufficient for the passenger and crew complement of 98 which she was allowed to convey.

National Railway Museum

was felt necessary to press the case for remedial action with the Admiralty under whose watchful eye they had to operate. They in turn contacted the Commander-in-Chief, Home Forces, on the matter. Eventually the SR was given permission to carry out the work, which was done in 1943 by James Dredging, Towage and Transport Co. of Southampton.

On 4th May, 1942 Cowes suffered terribly from an air raid by the Luftwaffe, the targets being the Saunders-Roe aircraft works and the shipyard of J.S. White. It was said that 69 tons of bombs actually fell in the target area.

The authorities quickly perceived that the anti-aircraft gun defences needed to be strengthened. Operation 'Lettered' was immediately mounted only to find that the 3.7 in. guns with their AEC Matador towing vehicle could not be conveyed on the Fishbourne route as the link-span was only capable of carrying 8 tons, so they had to use the Lymington route instead. The matter was soon followed up with the SR Marine Department, which stated that currently *Wootton* was undergoing overhaul and arrangements could be made to stregthen the link-span so as to permit the movement across of vehicles up to 15 tons, but it would cost £400. This expenditure was promptly agreed and by July the necessary authorisation had been given by the military for similar work to be carried out on the *Fishbourne* and *Hilsea* when they were next in for repairs. A spin-off was the fact that the passenger numbers could be increased to 200.

The operations in connection with 'D' Day resulted in a certain number of foot-passengers being redirected to this route for a week whilst the paddle steamers were withdrawn for ferrying troops between the mainland and their ship. While this was going on, junior clerk G.D. Henley, who normally worked at Ryde Pier booking office, had each day to go first from his home on the outskirts of Ryde, pick up a £5 float together with some single tickets to Portsmouth, and then cycle to Fishbourne, a distance of about four miles, and assist in the work there. Otherwise the service continued to operate as usual, though because of falling demand the Tuesday trip at mid-day had been discontinued.

Whilst all these wartime activities had been going on, the SR considered in 1944 that the time was opportune to decide on peacetime operations and in particular what shipbuilding should be undertaken during the next five years. The project committee's recommendations, which were adopted, speak for themselves:

> Apart from a few Saturdays in the summer, the pre-war fleet of three craft were sufficient to lift the traffic, and on other days of the week much additional traffic could have been conveyed. More vessels could not usefully be employed without enlargement of the terminal facilities at Wootton Creek. There have been no losses to date, and *no recommendation is made for new construction.*

A minor incident did however occur on 16th January, 1945 when *Hilsea* came in contact with a government dockyard craft shortly after leaving the Camber. Damage was estimated at £1,500 and action was taken by the SR to reclaim this amount from the vessel's owners. Seven months later *Hilsea* was involved in another incident. This happened on 31st July while she was passing through

MV Fishbourne on slipway for repairs

The car ferries used on the Portsmouth-Fishbourne route were of very simple construction and not suitable for the conveyance of heavy army lorries so in 1942 the decision was taken to improve the strength of the link-span from 8 to 15 tons capacity. The photograph taken on the slip at Dumbarton clearly shows the double twin screws and rudders mounted so as not to foul the slipways.

C. Grasemann

the Swashway on passage from Portsmouth to Fishbourne and struck a submerged object said to be part of PS *Portsdown*. The vessel was holed, but by dint of effort the Captain did manage to beach her near Southsea, and all the passengers got ashore safely, along with some horses. The underwater obstruction, which had caused damage estimated at £1,500, was removed by the Admiralty and the vessel sent to Southampton for repairs, which were not completed until the end of August. In the intervening period *Wootton* covered the service leaving *Fishbourne* to run to/from Lymington.

The crew shortage, as mentioned in the previous chapter on the paddle steamers, also affected the car ferries. So much so that only one vessel was worked, but with recourse to overtime it was possible to run an additional trip on a Saturday afternoon. On the clerical side there was a backlog of correspondence in the Broad Street offices at Portsmouth, which was eventually overcome by recruitment to fill existing vacancies and extensive overtime. On the operational side it was found desirable to transfer the tomato traffic from the Island to the car-ferry in preference to it being manhandled on the paddle steamer route. In the opposite direction there were problems with lorry loads of food for the Island, but this was resolved by allocating one space on each trip for a food lorry, which space could easily be offered to a waiting motorist if no lorry appeared.

Back in 1942 the SR had given an undertaking to modify the link-spans on the two other car-ferries when they were next in workshops. *Hilsea* had the alterations made when she was in for repairs following the incidents mentioned earlier, but *Fishbourne* had carried on without the need for attention and in consequence the alterations to this vessel had not been made when the War ended. The Docks & Marine Manager examined this situation, taking into account the observations made by the Project team involved with the five year building programme, together with the need for her to be more suitable for the Lymington-Yarmouth route, and put forward to the General Manager the following proposal:

	Description	*Estimated Cost*
(a)	Extension of prows by 3 ft and conversion to electrical operation to avoid risks of stranding on slipways and to facilitate mooring	£6,220
(b)	Replacement of three of the four hand-operated anchor mooring capstans by power-operated ones	£1,530
(c)	Provision of additional buoyant apparatus to increase passenger carrying capacity from 99 to 199	£250
		£8,000

This was agreed on 6th October, 1945 and eventually the works were completed in March 1947.

The change from war to peace had a downturn effect on revenue as more could be made from the conveyance of lorries than cars. The following figures show this trend:

MV Wootton on slipway at Portsmouth
This photograph taken just before the end of the War in April 1945 shows MV *Wootton* on Vosper's slipway in the Camber at Portsmouth. The wartime protection to the wheelhouse is clearly visible. In the foreground is a magnificent steam-driven Admiralty pinnace. *Vosper Thorneycroft*

	Cars		Lorries		Livestock	
1944	2,356		8,140		153	
1945	7,371		4,360		470	
	+ 5,015	(+ 212%)	- 3,780	(- 47%)	+ 317	(+ 207%)

	Passengers	Parcels	Freight	Livestock	Total
	£	£	£	£	£
1944	1,435	2,716	34,060	74	38,285
1945	1,795	8,585	19,082	109	29,571
	+ 360	+5,869	- 14,978	+ 35	8,714
	(+ 25%)	(+ 216%)	(- 44%)	(+ 47%)	(- 23%)

So the profitability of this route had to await the end of petrol rationing before it would exceed the 1938 figure of 23,217 for the number of cars carried.

MV Hilsea in Portsmouth Harbour
MV *Hilsea* is shown here in her peacetime guise with the Gosport passenger ferry terminal in the distance. The limited amount of covered accommodation is apparent though in fine weather the 55 min. journey could be very pleasant.   *World Ship Society*

Launch of PS Freshwater at Cowes 3rd May, 1927
PS *Freshwater* was the only genuine Isle of Wight ship, having been built for the Lymington-Yarmouth route by J. Samuel White of Cowes. It is difficult to recognise her as she was launched without paddle wheels or funnel.

Cowes Maritime Museum

Chapter Four

The Lymington-Yarmouth Service

Words perhaps cannot adequately describe the idyllic nature of the route from Lymington to Yarmouth on the Isle of Wight, (a distance just short of four miles), especially after the passing of the SR's Act in 1936 which heralded great improvements in the mode of transport across to the western part of the Island. Gone were the old tow boats on which cars, etc. precariously rested and in their place in 1938 came the great new roll-on roll-off ferry built by Denny's of Dumbarton and aptly named *Lymington*. Even the German propulsion unit was totally different as it enabled the Captain to move the craft in any direction desired. Small wonder that she soon earned the *nom de mer* 'Crab Ship'.

The three ships which served the route on the outbreak of war could best be described as having the best of the old and new combined.

Name	Built	Knots	Draught	Fuel	Cars	Passenger Certificate (winter)
PS *Solent*	1902	11	5 ft 6 in.	Coal	nil	390
PS *Freshwater*	1927	12	5 ft 8 in.	Coal	nil	436
MV *Lymington*	1938	9	5 ft 8 in.	Oil	16	200

Staffing of the vessels was as under:

Crew	Solent	Freshwater	Lymington
Master	1	1	1
Mate	1	1	1
Seamen (ABs)	2	2	3
Engineer	1	1	1
Fireman	2	2	-
Greaser	-	-	1
Steward	1	1	1
Stewardess	1	1	2
Boy	-	1	-
TOTAL	9	10	10

At Yarmouth there is a slipway by the entrance to the harbour to which a dredged channel of 9 ft was made by the Yarmouth Harbour Commissioners in 1938. Paddle steamers normally used the wooden pier.

At Lymington the layout of the Pier station had been improved with the provision of a short siding on which coal wagons could be stabled for bunkering the two paddle steamers. Fuel oil was dealt with on the same siding, but in the early days of the War the Petroleum Board erected an emergency tank on the site of what is now the ferry operator's offices. Livestock conveyance was restricted to the 07.40 and 09.15 sailings to the Island with two similar return services. As this movement was 'on the hoof' considerable cleaning of

PS Freshwater leaving Lymington Pier before the 1936 reconstruction
In 1936 the Southern Railway decided that the old system of barges with cars precariously perched on them was out of date. Therefore a slipway was constructed for use by MV *Lymington*, but PS *Freshwater* remained as a reserve in case of breakdowns before being transferred to Weymouth to act as an Examination vessel in 1940. *E.A. Sweetman*

Lymington Pier station under reconstruction 1937
In 1936 the Southern Railway took the decision in conjuction with the proposed introduction of MV *Lymington* to upgrade the facilities at Lymington Pier. The outline shows the proposed extension to the station building. Alongside the quay is James & Co.'s bucket dredger from Southampton. *British Railways*

the decks would have been required after these sailings. The SR's decision at a later stage in the design to fit Voith Schneider propellors resulted in their being installed at 22 degrees to the horizontal, which adversely affected the propellor blade bearings. In addition the inclined installation took the blades very close to the ship's side and they often sustained damage through contact with the banks of the Lymington river. Nevertheless, despite her problems, she proved adequate for the task and the capital investment of £31,633 would seem to have been justified.

At the commencement of the War, to forestall action by U-boats the Admiralty made an order prohibiting the lighting of navigation beacons, and in consequence all services after dark on this route ceased. The Sunday working which continued until near the end of September was normally covered by one of the paddle steamers. This service was reintroduced in May 1940 and lasted till September and continued in like fashion till after the end of the war. Even before the start of the war, the problems with the propellors on the *Lymington* caused great difficulties, especially for Fred Howland, who was the vessel's Engineer. Time and time again he had to nurse her back to Lymington and then place her on the grid to the east of the pier and await low tide so that the unit could be inspected.

This sort of problem affected Fred's domestic arrangements as he lived at Eastleigh, and it often meant he was very late home. Eventually the authorities decided he must live nearer his work, so he moved to Lymington. As is often the case with mechanical troubles of this nature involving new equipment, the English concessionaires - E.C. Goldworthy & Co. of Weybridge (now Aldershot) - had to attend with German engineers - one of whom was later convicted of being a spy and shot at Southsea Castle in 1941! One spare unit was kept in the Marine Workshops at Southampton Docks and it often fell to Assistant Marine Engineer Alexander Graham Liston, who was awarded an MBE for his services, to drive with his cousin John, a fitter Engineer (whose parents were farmers at Freshwater) through the New Forest at night with only cat's eyes to guide them to the stricken ship. Only by this sort of human exertion was the vessel kept in service. The other ferry engineer at Lymington - Charles Clark - often helped out.

Fortunately, the only lengthy period for which she was out of service in 1940 took place between 21st February and 19th March, with the vessel achieving an almost unblemished record at work in 1941. To the military she was an essential link with the Island since she was the only vessel which had a link span capable of carrying 15 tons. However when totally given over to military use her loading could be any one of the following configurations:

(a)   600 troops
(b)   14 Bren gun carriers plus 200 troops
(c)   14 8-cwt vehicles plus 200 troops
(d)   Ten 15-cwt vehicles plus 200 troops
(e)   Ten 5-ton vehicles plus 200 troops
(f)   Eight 3-ton vehicles plus 200 troops

PS Freshwater 25th July, 1939
During the evacuation from Dunkirk PS *Freshwater* made her way to Sheerness, but seems to have arrived too late to take an active role. At the end of 1940 she was requisitioned by the Navy and spent most of her time as an examination ship outside the ports of Weymouth and Portland. Eventually in 1945 she resumed her peacetime role and was retained after nationalisation until 1957.

Portsmouth Record Office

As mentioned earlier, she did not operate on a Sunday, but the military did request her presence on 12th May and 7th July, 1940, though in the following year she managed to escape these extra duties. The latter date involved the movement of the 2nd Royal Northumberland Fusiliers, but their stay was short-lived as they left by the same route to the mainland on 6th September, having been replaced by the Royal West Kent Regiment who had travelled over to the Island on the ferry the previous day. The 8th December saw the 2nd Bn Royal Fusiliers leave the Island in similar fashion. The military 'Rail Transport Officer' for movements on the ferries and rail workings in the immediate area was Captain Sidney Harding, who held a Wartime Commission, as in peacetime he worked in the Excursion Department of the SR's district office at Southampton and thus was well versed in the transport situation in the area.

The Island authorities were acutely aware that, following the fall of France, they might be the subject of considerable bombing, not to mention the very real possibility of an invasion; and therefore wished to ensure that adequate transport to the mainland was available for the evacuation of the injured. Following consultation with the Ministry of Health, a meeting was held with the SR on 22nd July, 1940, at which it was agreed that the most suitable route was that between Yarmouth and Lymington as MV *Lymington* could convey 90 stretcher cases, as well as 200 walking wounded. A full scale test was to have taken place on 17th August, but never took place, and there the matter rested.

The impact of the evacuation of Dunkirk was barely noticed on this route, though PS *Freshwater* did make her way to Sheerness, where on 1st June, 1940 she was joined by Sub-Lieut Moran Caplat, RNVR. As to involvement, little is known; perhaps she arrived too late to take part in the proceedings.*

The old PS *Solent*, built for the London & South Western Railway way back in 1902, had already been involved in a shooting incident in peacetime. Owing to excessive speed on the Lymington river she caused wash that broke the mooring lines of several dinghies, so enraging the owner that he fired both barrels of his shotgun into the canvas around the uncovered wheelhouse.

Much later in 1940 she was laid up in Southampton Docks at No. 10 berth in the Inner Harbour. She was there on 26th September, when the Germans bombed the docks and as a result Warehouse 'D' which was adjacent caught fire. Now it just so happened that the SR's MV *Autocarrier* was berthed nearby and her Chief Officer - H.F. Breuily - noticed that blazing timbers had fallen on to the paddle steamer's deck. Realising that if the deck caught fire the ship would soon be ablaze as she was of timber construction, he quickly went aboard and put the blazing pieces of wood over the side and thereby saved the ship.

Following the fall of France, the Admiralty were most concerned to ensure that no surprise attack took place on any south coast port or that a 'Q' ship should surreptitiously enter port and blow herself up, thereby causing extensive damage to ships and dockside facilities in the harbour. To overcome this problem a ship was to be located outside each port to check on the bona fide nature of each vessel seeking entry. To start with the Navy at Portland had two ships - *Empress* and *Victoria* - to cover the port of Weymouth, but it soon became apparent to the authorities that they were not really suitable for the purpose. Accordingly a request was made to the SR on 21st October, 1940 to make PS

---

* This was no doubt in sharp contrast to her involvement with the Navy Review on 20th May, 1937.

PS Solent

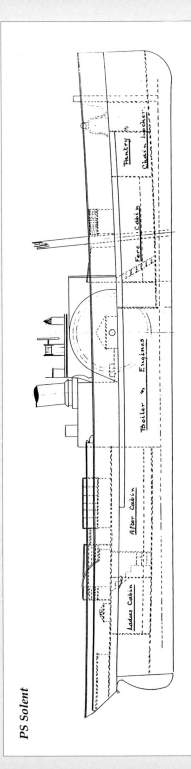

PS Solent

This vessel was constructed by Mordey, Carney Ltd of Southampton in 1902 for the London & South Western Railway being used on the Lymington-Yarmouth route where she stayed for most of the War. Following the arrival of MV *Farringford* in 1948 she was withdrawn.

PRO Rail Collection

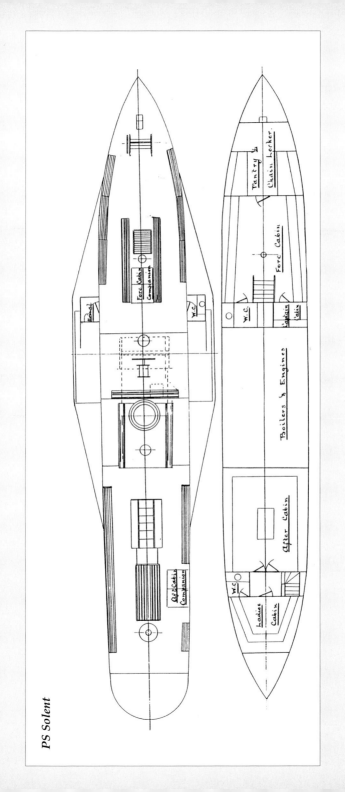

PS Solent

PS Freshwater leaving the pier at Yarmouth, Isle of Wight
Before the advent of MV *Lymington* with its roll-on roll-off facility passengers used the pier at Yarmouth, only cars and other freight traffic being dealt with on the quays.   *E.F. Toogood*

Yarmouth IoW aerial photograph 1940
In 1940 the German Luftwaffe took a number of aerial photographs of the island which were published in a booklet to help identification as a part of Operation 'Sealion' (see also photograph on page 40).   *Alderney Museum*

PS Solent at Lymington Town landing pontoon
PS *Solent*, built for the London & South Western Railway in 1902, is shown here laid up adjacent to the old landing pontoon by Lymington Town station in June 1947. She was taken out of use when the SR introduced MV *Lymington* onto the route in 1938. She was the second boat on the Lymington-Yarmouth route throughout the War and survived the bombing on 26th September, 1940 whilst at Southampton for annual overhaul, etc.
G.E. Kiltvington

PS Freshwater with sail assistance in Lymington River
The need to avoid damage to other craft in the Lymington River necessitated ships to proceed at a slow speed and sometimes this created problems with steerage hence the assistance that could be given by the use of a small sail.
National Railway Museum

Freshwater immediately available for this purpose. As she was the only spare ship the SR had at its disposal to cover services to the Island in the event of failure, the SR objected and lodged an objection with the Shipping Department. The Minister of War Transport decided on 7th November that the ship should be released, but only on 'condition that she is immediately available to evacuate hospital cases or evacuees from the Isle of Wight should invasion or other emergency render this necessary'. The SR took the view that the latter sentence meant within 24 hours if one of their ships on the Lymington-Yarmouth route was subjected to a major failure, but fortunately it was never necessary to take up this option, although it did result in PS *Solent* being brought back into the working.

No more was PS *Freshwater* to mingle with the Navy's four Auxiliary Patrol vessels - *Islanda*, *John Vander*, *Lotis* and *Kayee* - at Yarmouth nor the RAF's rescue boat *King Duck* as she sped out of harbour to save an airman who had to ditch into the sea. Instead she made her way to Cosens & Co. Ltd, Ship & Yacht repairers at Weymouth where she was quickly fitted out for her new role to wallow on the high sea. By mid-December she was sharing her new duties with PS *Consul* who within a few months was replaced by PS *Monarch*, both being owned by Messrs Cosens. To help with putting sailors aboard incoming vessels etc., she had two tenders - *Arlen* and *Marina* - assisted for a time by 'B3'. The departure of this spare paddle steamer helped to reduce the loss which was incurred on this route in 1940 even though the SR received an annual hire fee of £2,220 plus £119 for organisational expenses.

Captains Wilkins and Woolgar operated the remaining ships, which were more than adequate for the purpose to judge from the daily loadings shown for two representative periods in *Appendix Six*, even allowing for the fact that 80 per cent of the passengers were either military or naval personnel. What it also shows is that during this period of the War only about 10 per cent of the people travelling to the Island used the Lymington-Yarmouth route.

Strangely enough, the Lymington-Yarmouth ferry operated outside the protection given to the Ports of Southampton and Portsmouth. This took the form of nets, large flotation buoys and large moving buoys having a centre gate, operated by naval gate ships. In the Needles channel this stretched from Burns Point some four miles east of Lymington to Hamstead Ledge near Newtown IOW, with land-based protection being given by the Bouldner battery only erected in 1922.

Over the years the SR had spent considerable sums in dredging the Lymington river, with its tortuous course and many moored yachts. Navigation can never have been easy so it is pleasing to record that the Lymington Harbour Commissioners had paid tribute to the navigating skill and consideration of the Masters of the railway vessels. As late as 1938, £5,130 had been spent on the river to maintain the desired depth of water at low tide, yet by 1941 there was a need to carry out further work. So, having regard to the fact the Navy and military authorities were the prime users of the service, the SR asked the Admiralty if they would provide financial assistance. The Lords Commissioners in October when placing the matter before the Commander-in-Chief, Home Forces, stated:

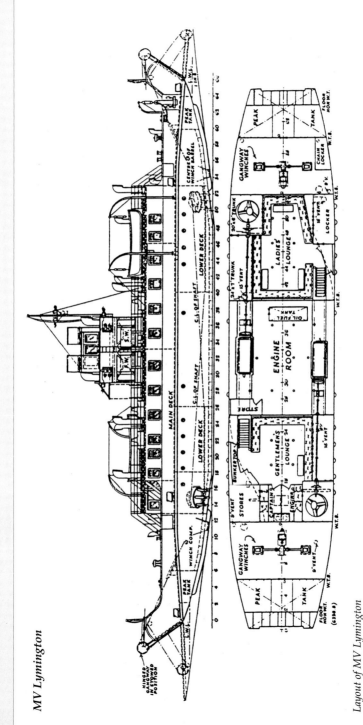

MV Lymington

Layout of MV Lymington

MV *Lymington* was the first car carrying vessel constructed in 1938 for the Lymington-Yarmouth service. Despite problems with her German propeller unit she was the mainstay of this route and provided the best means for moving heavy military vehicles to and from the Isle of Wight. After the War she continued there until 1974 when she was transferred to Scotland.

A. Brown

MV Lymington

There is no naval requirement for this dredging, but certain arrangements made for reinforcement of the Island in the event of invasion, might be prejudiced if the work is not done. It is understood that no difficulty is anticipated in transporting men, but that if artillery and tanks had to be sent, the security of the Island might be impaired, since, apart from any landing craft which may be available, the ferries between Portsmouth and Wootton Creek (Fishbourne), and Lymington and Yarmouth, are the only means of transport available.

Eleven days later the military replied as follows:

It is considered that it is not likely to be possible to use WOOTTON CREEK as a landing place for reinfocements during operations, and therefore from the Military point of view no dredging is necessary in that channel. Therefore I am of the opinion that for military reasons any dredging necessary to keep the channels of Lymington open at all states of the tide should be carried out, and it is therefore requested that you inform Their Lordships accordingly.

The matter was then discussed with the SR who arranged for the work to be carried out by James Dredging Towage and Transport Co. of Southampton at a cost of £13,278 of which the railway paid 25 per cent (£3,320).

No sooner had the dredging been carried out than the Lymington route came into prominence for, as recorded in the previous chapter, Cowes experienced a terrible air raid on 4th May, 1942. The upshot was that operation 'Lettered' was mounted almost straightaway, which required the transfer of the 64th Heavy Anti-Aircraft Regiment with its 24 3.7 AA guns together with its AEC Matador towing units from Manchester and Leeds to the Island. In addition the 19th Light Anti-Aircraft (LAA) unit with its 96 Oerlikons (20 mm) came from Chippenham and the 98th LAA from Liverpool with its slightly larger 48 mm guns, eight of which were to be based at Yarmouth to defend the ferry. MV *Fishbourne* was moved across temporarily to Lymington to assist. By 15th May the shipment work had been completed and *Lymington* once again had been able to demonstrate her worth, which included working on three successive Sundays. The move had brought home to the military the importance of this route so arrangements were made to provide a 40 mm Bofors gun to defend Lymington Pier from air attack and it remained there until 24th April, 1944.

Back in September 1940 the SR had given concrete protection to the wheelhouse on the *Lymington* and *Freshwater* and supplied a Lewis gun. The latter armament on the *Lymington* was not used until the evening of Monday 10th August, 1942 when, whilst working the 18.05 Lymington-Yarmouth service, she was machine-gunned by a lone German raider five minutes out from the slipway. Chief Engineer Fred Howland recalls the memorable occasion:

I was sitting down in the engine room, along with a greaser, at the time and suddenly something fell down at the bottom of the engine room ladder. We got up and found it to be the glass cover of an electric light fitting, so we went up and found a hole where a bullet had gone through the bulkhead and knocked off the light fitting at the engine room entrance. That bullet actually ended up in the engine room but another went through the seat of a bicycle leaning against the ship's side. Of course we hadn't heard a thing down in the engine room and had no idea of what was going on.

In fact, quite a lot had been going on, and at the first sign of trouble, when the Heinkel aircraft HE111 of 2/RG27 squadron swooped down towards *Lymington*, deck hand G. Stickles dashed on to the bridge to man the Lewis gun and his quick return of fire may well have prevented the attack from being pressed home. Mr Stickles was subsequently warmly praised for his prompt actions and devotion to duty and received a number of official letters of commendation, including one from the General Manager, Eustace Missenden. Never again was the vessel to be attacked by German aircraft.

Preparations for the invasion of France started early in 1943 when the Admiralty examined the slipway facilities at Lymington and decided they were too narrow for two Landing Craft Tanks. Accordingly through the Ministry of War Transport the SR was asked to double its width and this was carried out at a cost of £5,000. In addition, shortly after Christmas the Railway Executive Committee advised that they had received 'intimation from Service Departments that in 1944 they might require the Lymington-Yarmouth service to be suspended from time to time for periods up to 72 hours'.

And there the matter rested until on 29th April, 1944 a telegram was received from the C-in-C Portsmouth which was not quite what had been expected. Instead of requisitioning MV *Lymington* the C-in-C stated that the Pier at Lymington would not be available between the hours of 13.30 and 22.00 on 1st May, presumably so that the slipway could be used for the loading of American tank landing craft which were to form part of Force 'J'. This severely curtailed the sailings, though one did take place at high tide, when it was possible to sail right up to the Town station and use the old facilities. Some time later on 19th May the SR was advised that PS *Solent* was to be requisitioned for special duties over two days for the transfer of troops from shore to ship under the control of the Sea Transport Officer at Southampton. A week later she carried out this commitment.

Whilst these day to day problems were being successfully overcome, senior management had turned their attention to any changes that might be necessary in the provision of ships on the Lymington route. The Committee appointed to report on a five-year building programme commented as follows:

The principal revenue from this route is from motor cars and commercial vehicles, and with the introduction of the MV *Lymington* in 1938 the traffic increased considerably. To cater adequately for the traffic which may be expected after the war a new vessel of the Lymington type to take road vehicles and passengers is recommended, but having regard to the unreliability of the present Voith-Schneider propellors an alternative form of propulsion should be investigated. The PS *Solent*, built in 1902, could then be sold.

The commercial justification rested on the fact that there had been a considerable increase in motor traffic by this route before the War, the 1938 carryings being 72 per cent over the 1937 and the 1939 carryings up to the outbreak of war showing a 107 per cent increase over the corresponding months in 1938. Indeed, it was their considered opinion that this trend would continue as the route is convenient for motorists from the Midlands to all places in the Isle of Wight. The route would also serve the proposed holiday centre at Farringford.

SOUTHERN RAILWAY.

TELEPHONE:
DORKING 3201.

E. J. MISSENDEN.
General Manager.

GENERAL MANAGER'S OFFICE,
DEEPDENE HOTEL,
DORKING, SURREY.

IN YOUR REPLY PLEASE
QUOTE THIS REFERENCE:
S.Pad.104.

31st August, 1942.

Dear Sir,

My attention has been drawn to the action
taken by you on the occasion of the recent aerial attack
on the m.f. "Lymington" and I hasten to commend you, not
only on the promptitude with which you returned the fire
of the enemy aircraft, but on your devotion to duty under
hazardous conditions.

Mr. G.Sticklee,
Deck Hand,
SOUTHAMPTON.

Yours faithfully,

FOR E. J. MISSENDEN.
GENERAL MANAGER.

John Eliot

DEPUTY GENERAL MANAGER.

Letter of appreciation to G. Sticklee
This letter was sent to G. Sticklee in recognition of his efforts with a Lewis gun on 10th August,
1942 when MV *Lymington* was strafed by a German Heinkel HE 111 of 2/KG 27 squadron.

A. Brown

MV Lymington during the War
MV *Lymington* is shown here in her wartime grey with the concrete protection atop of the
wheelhouse which was added in September 1940. She boasted a Ladies' Lounge, and a lounge
and a refreshment room for first-class passengers (officers), with similar facilities for third class
passengers (other ranks).

A. Brown

LONDON, BROCKENHURST, LYMINGTON, and YARMOUTH

(Service liable to alteration)

Miles (from Brockenhurst)	Down	mrn		mrn		mrn		mrn		aft		aft A		aft H		aft C
	Waterloo 324 ....dep.	2 40	..	5 40	..	9 30	..	11 30	..	1 30	..	3 30	..			4 35
	Southampton Cent.324 "	6 18	..	7 58	..	1134	..	1 25	..	3 22	..	4 27	..	5 36	..	6 22
	Brockenhurst ....dep.	7 4	..	8 34	..	12 8	..	1 55	..	4 1	..	5 12	..	6 55	..	6 56
	Lymington Pier .... { arr.	7 24	..	8 48	..	1215	..	2 14	..	4 14	..	5 26	..	7 9	..	7 9
	{ dep.	7 40	..	9 15	..	1230	..	2 15	..	4 20	..	5 40	..	7 15	..	7 15
	Yarmouth Slipway ..arr.	8 10	..	9 45	..	1 0	..	2 45	..	4 50	..	6 10	..	7 45	..	7 45

Miles (from Lymington)	Up	mrn		mrn		aft		aft		aft		aft		aft N
	Yarmouth Slipway ..dep.	3 25	..	10 40	..	1 25	..	2 55	..	5 0	..	6 25	..	7 55
	Lymington Pier .... { arr.	9 0	..	11 10	..	1 55	..	3 25	..	5 30	..	6 55	..	8 25
	(above) { dep.	9 5	..	11 22	..	2 12	..	3 32	..	5 35	..	7 34	..	8 27
	Brockenhurst 324 .....arr.	9 22	..	11 40	..	2 28	..	3 49	..	5 51	..	7 51	..	8 43
	Southampton Cent.330arr.	9 55	..	12 16	..	4 19	..	6 16	..	8 36	..	9 30	..
	Waterloo 330 .... "	12 9	..	2 19	..	6 36	..	8 37	..	1126	..	3155	..

A or I Not after 25th September **H** Saturdays only.   Not after 28th August

C Saturdays excepted. Not after 27th August   **N or I** Not after 28th August

---

LYMINGTON and YARMOUTH.

The ferry vessel "Lymington" has been specially constructed for the conveyance of motor vehicles (which run on and off the vessel under their own power without reversing).

These will be accepted on the ferry vessel on every passage (with certain exceptions as shown in the schedule of services).

Traffic must be upon the respective slipways ready to load half-an-hour before the advertised times. Vehicles, horses, and live stock must be in charge of senders' or owners' servant, who must accompany them.

Animals, other than Dogs, are not conveyed on Sundays. The passages available for such animals are:—Lymington, dep. 7A40 a.m. and 9.15 a.m. (Mondays excepted), Yarmouth Slipway, dep. 8A25 a.m. and 1.25 p.m.

A—To November 13th, 1943, and again commencing February 14th, 1944.

Senders or owners of motor cars, etc., by the Ferry Vessel take upon themselves all risk of conveyance and of loading and unloading, as the Company will not be responsible for loss, damage, or delay, however caused, of or to any vehicle, accessories therein or thereon, or other property therein or belonging thereto.

Alterations and additions will be made in the above services during Easter, Whitsuntide, and Christmas periods. It is advisable, especially during holiday periods and the summer months, to reserve accommodation in both directions as long in advance as possible. No charge is made for the reservation, and communications should be addressed to the Station Master at Lymington (Telephone No. 7), or the Station Master, Yarmouth (Telephone No. 21.9).

RATES FOR MOTOR CARS, ETC.
(at Owner's Risk), via Lymington and Yarmouth.

Books containing 4 Return Motor Car Tickets, at reduced rates, are obtainable. For full particulars, see above.	Single.	Return (A) (Available for 3 months)	(A) Week End (Friday to Tuesday).	(A) Day Return (Week Day).
	£ s. d.	£ s. d.	£ s. d.	£ s. d.
Motor Cars { Not exceeding 10 feet 6 inches in length	17 4	1 11 9	1 5 11	1 3 3
Over 10 feet 6 inches in length and not exceeding 14 feet in length	1 5 6	2 2 3	1 18 2	1 14 1
Over 14 feet in length	1 17 2	3 2 8	2 15 8	2 9 8
Motor Tri-Car ..	15 5	1 7 11	1 2 1	1 0 6
Motor Cycle and Side Car (accompanied)..	5 10	10 5	8 8	7 8
Motor Cycle (accompanied) ..	3 5½	6 4	5 2	4 8
Motor Car Trailers	12 9½	1 5 7	19 2	17 0
Caravans attached to Motor Cars ..	— At Motor Car Rates—			
Cyc-Autos (E)	1 6	(E) 2 4	..	..
Bicycles (accompanied)	0 11½	..	..	..
Persons accompanying Traffic (Third Class)	2 1	4 2	2 9	2 9

A—The return halves of these tickets may be used, if so desired, via Fishbourne and Portsmouth. (E) Not available via Fishbourne and Portsmouth.

A special reduced rate of a single fare and a third for the return journey is available for bona-fide **Commercial Travellers** and their Motor Cars between any one Monday and Friday.
For rates for animals, furniture, etc., see other announcements.

☞ Senders or Owners of Motor Cars, &c., by the Ferry Vessel take upon themselves all risk of conveyance and of loading and unloading, as the Company will not be answerable for Accidents, Loss, or Damage done to any vehicles, accessories therein or thereon or other property therein or belonging thereto.

This extract from the Southern Railway timetable shows the effect of boats being restricted to the hours of daylight. Surprisingly, despite travel restrictions, mention is made of the need for advance bookings during holiday periods.

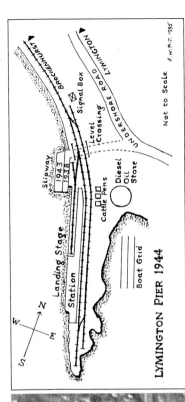

LYMINGTON PIER 1944

Landing Stage

Station

Slipway

1943
1938

Signal Box

Level Crossing

Cattle Pens

Diesel Oil Store

Boat Grid

UNDERSHORE ROAD

BROCKENHURST

LYMINGTON

Not to Scale

E.W.P.T. 1995

N
W — E
S

Above: The facilities at Lymington enabled the car ferry to be berthed end-on to the slipway with a paddle steamer alongside the slipway. The station had a 310 ft wooden platform, with a canopy over 210 ft of its length. This could accommodate a five-coach train, but if need arose a nine-coach train could be accommodated, although troops then had to walk through part of the train.

G. Pryer

Left:
Lymington, 1st May, 1944
Just before D-Day for the Invasion of Europe the American Air Force took a number of photographs depicting the embarkation areas. Lymington took only a small part, but the location of the remaining small ships can be clearly seen, the number being in sharp contrast to the present day.

USAF/National Monuments Record

Even before the War had ended the SR took the next step in February 1945 and had consultations with William Denny & Brothers Ltd to determine the exact form the new vessel should take. Matters moved quickly and, in the following month, this had been worked out and agreed by the Board, with the result that an application was made to the Ministry of War Transport for a 'Permit to Contract' to be issued. This was soon forthcoming and in accordance with SR practice, the quotation of £94,850 from Denny's had been accepted. The firm took note of their long connection with the SR and limited their profit to 7 per cent. The problem of the propulsion unit for the new vessel (MV *Farringford*) had been fully explored and, following demonstrations with another of Denny's ships on the Firth of Forth, the decision was taken to instal independent paddle wheels with diesel-electric drive under bridge control. The following table sets out the differences between the MV *Lymington* and the MV *Farringford*.

Particulars	MV Lymington	MV Farringford
Length (ft)	148	168
Breadth (ft)	37	48
Draft (ft)	5.75	6
Gross Tons	274	500
Deadweight Tons	45	95
Speed (knots)	9	10.5
Passengers	200	320
Cars	16	32

The formal contract was not signed until 7th August, 1946 and, following delivery to Southampton, she entered service on 4th March, 1948.

The case for the new vessel was based on a sound financial judgement, bearing in mind that the SR expected its ships to last for 25 years. Assuming that the projected traffic growth lived up to expectations and that the operating costs were contained within a reasonable level, the contract figure, even using the 1945 net receipt figure of £8,174 meant that after 12 years the initial cost of the ship could be written off, but in reality a much better return on capital investment was achieved, as the profit in 1946 was £26,019 and in 1947 was even higher at £30,749. This was quite an achievement and came about because 19p of every £1 received was profit!

The year 1945 was difficult as the service given below had to be operated without PS *Freshwater*.

	WEEKDAYS, 7th May to 29th September, 1945, only.												SUNDAYS, 20th May to 16th September, 1945, only.			
	F	F	★ SO	★ SO F	F	F	★ SO	F	F	F	F		F	F		F
	a.m.	a.m.	a.m.	a.m.	p.m.	p.m.	p.m.	p.m.	p.m.	p.m.		a.m.	p.m.		p.m.	
Lymington Pier . . . . Boat dep.	7 40	9 15	10C15	11C20	12D30	2 15	3C30	4 20	5 40	7J15		10 0	12 45	.	4 30	.
Yarmouth Pier Head ......Boat arr.	....	....	....	....	....	....	....	....	....	....		....	....	.	....	...
Yarmouth Slipway ....Boat ,,	8 10	9 45	10C45	11C50	1D 0	2 45	4C 0	4 50	6 10	7J45		10 30	1 15	.	5 0	.

	F	F	★ SO	B F	F	F	★ SO	F	F	F	F		F		F	F
	a.m.	a.m.	a.m.	p.m.	p.m.	p.m.	p.m.	p.m.	p.m.	p.m.		a.m.		p.m.	p.m.	
Yarmouth Slipway . . . Boat dep.	8E30	10 40	11C20	12C30	1D30	2 55	4C45	5 0	6 25	7J55		10 40		2 0	5 30	.
Yarmouth Pier Head ......Boat ,,	...	...	...	...	...	...	...	...	...	...		...		...	...	...
Lymington Pier . . . . Boat arr.	9 0	11 10	11C50	1C 0	2D 0	3 25	5C15	5 30	6 55	8J25		11 10		2 50	6 0	.

★—Service performed by Steamer.   C—Will apply on Saturdays only July 7th to September 25th, 1945, only.
D—Service performed by Steamer on Saturdays, 7th July, to 15th September, 1945.   E—Advertised 8.25 a.m.
F—Ferry Vessel.   J—Until September 15th, 1945, only.

PS Freshwater alongside the enlarged slipway at Lymington, 12th August, 1951
As part of the facilities for the Invasion of Europe, the decision was taken in 1943 to double the width of the slipway so that it could accommodate two landing craft. PS *Freshwater* was berthed alongside when not required for traffic purposes adjacent to where she was swung on completion of each round trip to the Island.

Author's Collection

She had in fact finished her commitment at Weymouth in July 1944 when she was sent on to Chatham. By the end of October she had been paid off by the Admiralty, and sent to Southampton. Initially it had been thought that the reconditioning needed to bring her up to peacetime standards could be carried out by Vosper's at Portsmouth, but this was found not to be possible. Similarly, there was no spare capacity at Southampton, so she was sent back to Weymouth. November 1945 saw her returned, but because of pressing commitments she was placed on the Portsmouth-Ryde route as from 8th December before taking up her peacetime role on the Lymington-Yarmouth route after the New Year.

The increased level of business in 1945 and 1946 is clearly demonstrated by the figures below:

Year	Passengers	Cars	Lorries	Livestock
1938	225,784	4,063	1,168	5,621
1944	114,439	2,849	9,798	1,482
1945	261,832	11,267	8,082	2,360
1946	343,600	24,381	8,616	2,637

The increased level of passengers could well have been due to the pulling power of the excellent beaches at Alum Bay, Colwill Bay, Freshwater Bay and Totland Bay. To this might be added the excellent transfer facilities at Lymington Pier, where the train pulls up alongside the boat, and at Yarmouth where a short stroll takes passengers to the bus loading point. The substantial car increase is perhaps somewhat surprising in view of the fact that petrol rationing was still very much in existence, but the beaches and leafy lanes on the Island were a great attraction and August, with its holiday-makers was understandably a peak month:

Year (August)	Cars
1938	1,042
1939	2,459
1945	3,124

These figures, and those above, demonstrate quite clearly that the decision to purchase a second car ferry, instead of a passenger boat, was fully justified.

It was not surprising to find that the authorities decided that PS *Solent* should spend most of her time at Portsmouth acting as spare vessel to cover PS *Merstone* and PS *Shanklin* in the event of failure until after the end of August when she returned to Lymington. The gap was filled initially by the car ferry MV *Wootton* and later by MV *Fishbourne* which remained there till after Easter 1946 and therefore covered the services shown in the timetable to be worked by a steamer. This reduced capacity for foot passengers by about 300 per sailing, but this was offset by an additional 8 spaces for cars. The net result was that passengers could be accommodated on the car ferries without the massive queuing problems experienced on the Portsmouth-Ryde route and in 1946 the situation was even better with both paddle steamers being available. To meet

Yarmouth Harbour 1953
The pier for the paddle steamers is shown, together with MV *Lymington* at the slipway. In the middle of the harbour are the dredger and tug of James Dredging of Southampton, which were used in the River Lym during the War. The cattle pens were just out of view on the right near the Coast Guard station.

E. Toogood

peak needs on summer Saturdays, rail travel was improved by the provision of a boat train which was run once each way between Lymington and Waterloo under special traffic arrangements.

The scenario concerning MV *Lymington* has all the hallmarks of more goings-on than have been recorded. Firstly, it would seem more than probable that behind-the-scenes activities took place over a lunch or at another suitable occasion between either SR senior management and/or a senior officer in Southern Command and a senior officer of the United States Air Force. Suffice to say that when the American Army captured the Voith works in Heidenheim, it had escaped being bombed. Furthermore, whatever may, or may not, have happened behind the scenes, it was fortunate for the SR that it was able to get very useful repairs carried out at the undamaged German factory, and through the German owners elicited the news that maps had been prepared which showed that the factory was not to be targeted as a case had been made out for its use in helping with the rehabilitation of Europe. As a result MV *Lymington* was able to enter her peacetime role and earn for herself the title of 'The Sound of Success', and it speaks volumes for her design that in 1995 the vessel is still afloat in Scotland. PS *Freshwater* was eventually scrapped in 1962 after 35 years service, but PS *Solent* still survives as Burt's Café alongside the A27 at Portchester, having relinquished her role as a ferry boat as long ago as 1948.

Today the ferry facilities have hardly changed. You can still sit on the top deck, partaking of coffee (or something stronger) from the buffet, and watch the myriad of yachts as you sail down the Lymington river.

At the time of 'D' Day the yacht moorings were restricted to a small area off the public slipway, with the remainder up river of the railway bridge, but the situation now is quite different thanks to the peaceful conditions of the last 50 years. Among so many signs of peace and prosperity, it might now be easy to forget the efforts of those who made it all possible through their hard work and sacrifice during the dark days of the war. The Southern Railway's ferry-boats played their part in this, and we should remember all the men who served on them, and in particular the men of PS *Portsdown* who lost their lives when the ship was mined in September 1941. Their sacrifice should never be forgotten.

MV Lymington near Wootton Creek 1960s
The relative size of the slipway at Wootton Creek can be gauged from this panoramic picture taken about 1960 when MV *Lymington* had been displaced from the Lymington-Yarmouth route. *British Railways*

Appendix One

Southern Railway
Active Operations in Isle of Wight

SECRET

On receipt of 'ACTIVE STATIONS SEA TRANSPORT' the Divisional Sea Transport Officer, Southampton, will take over control of all civil Ships and craft suitable for operation between the Mainland and Isle of Wight and will use them in accordance with the circumstances prevailing.

'Action Stations Sea Transport' will be passed by the D.S.T.O to Southern Railway Docks Control, Southampton - Telephone 76241 or 3415.

Docks Control immediately to inform:

(1). Docks & Marine Manager and Assistant Docks & Marine Manager.

(2). Divisional Marine Manager, Southampton, who will proceed immediately to Movement Control, D.S.T.O's Office at South Western Hotel, Southampton, Docks Telephone 730. P.O. Telephone 3607 or 3678.

(3). Supt. Marine Engineer, who will arrange that Engineers are available for all Southern Railway Ships, also that any of the Company's steamers which may be at Southampton are prepared for service at the earliest possible moment, advising the Divisional Marine Manager, Southampton, at the Movement Control, South Western Hotel, of the position and also of the numbers of men and grades required to man the vessel or vessels.

(4). Divisional Marine Manager, Portsmouth, (Office hours 7.30 am to 9.0 pm - Company's telephone or Portsmouth 6077. After 9.0 pm Havant 486 (Mr Pelly's residence) and Emsworth 460 (Mr Macdonald)).

(5). Station Master, Lymington. Company's line or Post Office Telephone 'Lymington 7'. (N.B. After 8.30 pm the most expeditious method of getting a message to Station Master, Lymington, is through Lymington Police, Telephone 'Lymington 18'.
An alternative method is through E.S.O, Lymington Pier, Telephone Lymington 231, or through H.Q. Military Movement Control, Southampton.

(6). Station Master, Yarmouth. Post Office Telephone 'Yarmouth 213'. Office hours 8.0 am to 6.30 pm (8.0 pm May 30th to August 30th). Private address 'Provident Villa', Station Road, Yarmouth, but after Office hours can best be contacted through Yarmouth Police - Telephone 'Yarmouth 216'. Alternative - Through Embarkation Officer, Yarmouth - Telephone 'Yarmouth (IoW) 2323'.

(7). Divisional Marine Manager, Southampton, will detail one Clerk (Mr Tucker) to report to Southern Railway Docks Control. If after Office hours contact can be made with him through the Police, Whaddon, Telephone 'Alderbury 208'. Private address - 'Clearbury View', Whaddon, near Salisbury.

Upon receipt of 'ACTION STATIONS SEA TRANSPORT' the Divisional Marine Manager, Portsmouth, will arrange for:

(1). One Clerk (Mr M. Strivens) to proceed to Cowes Control (H.M.S. *Vectis*, Cowes) - Mr Strivens' home address is 18 Milward Road, Ryde, Isle of Wight.

(2). Advise Southampton Docks Control of the position of all vessels, following this up as quickly as possible with information as to crews available, and numbers and grades required to be provided by Naval Authorities to enable all available ships to be manned.

Docks Control to pass this information to Divisional Marine Manager, Southampton, at Movement Control (D.S.T.O's Office, South Western Hotel, Docks Telephone 730 or Post Office Telephone 3678 or 3607).

Under certain circumstances the Control may be transferred to H.Q. Military Movement Control, Southampton. Post Office Telephone 2531, or by direct line from Docks Telephone Exchange.

(3). Advise Assistant for Isle of Wight (Mr Gardner), Office hours 9.0 am to 5.0 pm Mondays to Fridays, 9.0 am to 12.00 m/day Saturdays - Telephone No. 'Newport, I. of W. 2429' - home address - 1, Sydney Terrace, Ryde, Telephone No. 2989. Station Master, Ryde, Telephone No. 'Ryde 2560' day or night. Clerk-in-Charge at Fishbourne (Mr Webb), Telephone No. 'Wootton Bridge 32' day or night.

Mr Webb will arrange for screened navigation lights to be lighted and placed in position in Wootton Creek if any move has to be made at night.

The Station Master, Lymington, will summon Masters and crews of both *Lymington* and *Solent* and arrange to light up *Solent*, and for all Shore staff to be on duty, reporting to Docks Control when arrangements are complete.

Foreman Cooper to be prepared to place shaded lights in Lymington River if any move has to be made at night, including arrangements for lights at Yacht Club.

The Station Master, Lymington, must arrange that contact can be made with the Harbour Master, Lymington, regarding lights on Yacht Club.

Foreman Cooper and one hand should be available throughout the operations to give assistance with the Company's motor launch to vessels navigating the river, and particularly to pilot the Portsmouth ferry if the move has to take place in darkness.

The Station Master, Yarmouth, must be prepared to receive and moor vessels either at the pierhead or slipway, and to arrange communication with the Harbour Master so that the Commissioners' staff will also be on duty.

The D.S.T.O., Southampton, will acquaint the S.N.O., Yarmouth, and if the operations have to proceed during the hours of darkness, the S.N.O.,Yarmouth, will arrange for the leading lights at Yarmouth to be lighted, and also one light indicating Yarmouth Pierhead to be in position.

The D.S.T.O., Southampton, will also make all arrangements necessary for navigation lights to be available for the Portsmouth/Ryde and Portsmouth/Fishbourne services if required.

Divisional Marine Manager, Southampton, and Mr Strivens, Divl. Marine Manager's Office, Portsmouth, will act as Liaison Officers at the two Government Controls (i.e. Southampton and Cowes), so far as the Southern Railway vessels are concerned, and will also assist the D.S.T.O. and Military Authorities as required.

On receipt of 'ACTION STATIONS SEA TRANSPORT' the undermentioned offices are to be continuously manned:

Supt. Marine Engineer, Southampton
Divl. Marine Manager, Southampton
Divl. Marine Manager, Portsmouth
Divl. Marine Manager, Fishbourne, I. of W.
Station Master, Ryde, I. of W.
Station Master, Lymington,
Station Master, Yarmouth, I. of W.

Throughout the operations all concerned must pass all useful information to Docks Control with as little delay as possible, and Docks Control will in turn pass to Docks & Marine Manager and to Divisional Marine Manager at D.S.T.O. Control.

In the event of South Western Hotel being out of action, the Control will be transferred to Southern Railway Docks Control, Southampton Docks. Telephone P.O. 76241 of 3415.

If neither of these positions is available the Control will transfer to Testwood School, Totton. Telephone Totton 7834.

Breakdown of Telephones

In the event of the breakdown of telephonic communications, messages to the Southampton Officials will have to be dealt with by despatch riders.

In the case of instructions for Portsmouth and the Isle of Wight, the messages should be passed to the Divisional Sea Transport officer (Duty Officer) for transmission by radio to the appropriate Naval or Military officer, to be re-transmitted to the individuals concerned.

Appendix Two

Dunkirk Operations
PS *Portsdown*

S/Lt R.H. Church, RNR
S/Lt M.V.H. Caplat, RNVR
(1st Lieut)

1st June	12.30		Left Sheerness for Dunkirk. RAF patrol aircraft encountered along the entire route to F.G. buoy
	21.50		*Abeam Dunkirk breakwater*
	22.05		Anchored off beach. Under shore bombardment. Embarked troops, using the ship's two dinghies. One of them sank on its 4th trip; the other later.
2nd June	03.00		In 1½ hours, a large motor boat had ferried 500 troops to the *Portsdown*.
	04.00	*ca*	Early dawn. Proceeded.
	04.50		1 mile west of Dunkirk breakwater, transferred about 1,000 troops from a French vessel which was aground.
	-		Transferred 25 troops from a motor boat, which declined a tow.
	-		Picked up Cdr J.C. Clouston, RN, and his party (about 12 in all) from a motor driven 'Naval pontoon boat'. Cdr Clouston ordered that she was to be abandoned.
	-		Obtained a course from the cr *Calcutta*.
	09.30	*ca*	*Arrived Ramsgate. Disembarked 168 BEF and 450 French troops.*

Total 618

(As *Portsdown* was not degaussed, she was not again used in 'Dynamo').

The following awards were made:

Mention in despatches

S/Lt R.H. Church, RNR	
E.R.A. 3rd cl	H. White
Sto P.O.	W. Ramel
L/Sig.	P.A. Kent
Ord. Sea.	A.T. Burton

Appendix Three

Dunkirk Operations
PS *Whippingham*

Lieut E. Reed, RNR

31st May	12.00	Arrived Ramsgate from Portsmouth. The *Whippingham* required fresh water, but as it then seemed likely that this would be the final trip, the pier master at Ramsgate (Capt E.F. Wharton RN), in order to save time, ordered her to fill up with salt water.
	13.45	Left Ramsgate for Dunkirk.
	16.30	*Off Malo beach*
	17.00/18.30	Made 3 unsuccessful attempts to put the ship's stern on the beach.
	18.30	Anchored
	21.30	Ordered to take troops off Dunkirk mole.
	22.00	Secured alongside the mole. Embarked troops
1st June	01.30	Completed the embarkation of 2,700 troops
		Overladen. Sponsons only about 12 inches above the water. Ship straddled by shell fire, which led to troops rushing over to the port side, causing a list of 20°. Chief Mechanician Ford checked the rush and moved the troops back to starboard thus preventing a disaster. Proceeded.
	08.00	Ramsgate. Ordered to Margate
	09.30	*Margate*
	11.30	*Disembarked 2,700 troops*

Total 2,700

The following awards were made:

DSM
   Ch. Mech. 2nd Cl. F A Ford

Appendix Four

Dunkirk Operations
PS *Sandown*

(J.20) P M/S (10th M.S.F.)   Actg Cdr K M Greig, RN
                                     S.O. 10th M.S.F.

27th May	21.00	Slipped, ships in company, the PM/S's *Gracie Fields, Medway Queen, Princess Elizabeth* and *Brighton Belle*.
28th May	02.00	*Passed Dunkirk* - heavy bombing and machine gunning in progress.
	03.15	Anchored off La Panne. Sent in all available boats with an ex-Belgian canal boat (the *Yser*) Assisted by the cr *Calcutta's* boats, embarked 600 BEF. Frequent air attacks.
	06.15	Proceeded alongside the cr *Calcutta* and transferred troops.

[About an hour later the *Sandown* apparently sailed from La Panne]

	12.30	While in company with the *Sandown*, the *Brighton Belle* struck a wreck off the Gull Light Buoy during an air attack and sank. All the crew and troops were rescued and tranferred to the *Sandown*, the *Medway Queen* and the ex-Belgian M/B *Yser*. Paymaster S/Lt W.J. Butler, RNVR of the Sandown was killed and 2 ratings wounded.
	14.30	*Arrived Margate. Disembarked 201 troops*.
	19.30	Returned to Dover.
29th May	05.30	Slipped and proceeded with the *Gracie Fields* to La Panne.
	14.30	*Anchored off La Panne*. Sent in all boats and embarked 800 troops during heavy bombing. Had to get under way twice. *Gracie Fields* reported sinking, after an attack off Middel Kerke Buoy.
	21.03	Dispatched the *Princess Elizabeth* to stand by her [in the meantime, however, the M/S *Pangbourne* had embarked the *Gracie Fields'* troops and taken her in tow].
	21.50	Proceeded with 800 British troops to Ramsgate.
30th May	05.00	*Arrived Ramsgate. Disembarked 860 troops*.
		Proceeded to Dover for coal and ammunition.
	21.00	Sailed from Dover
31st May	02.35	Anchored off N Goodwins in response to an SOS from the dfr *Golden Gift* which was aground with 250 troops on board.
		Took off the troops in the motor boat (five
	06.45	trips) and returned to Ramsgate to disembark them.

[The tug *Doris* reports that at 0800 she was ordered to take off troops from a minesweeper off Ramsgate (believed to be the *Sandown*) She landed them at Ramsgate east pier. Ramsgate report, however, states that only 90 were landed.]

	11.00	Proceeded to Bray. Shelled by Nieuport batteries off Middel Kerke Buoy.

	14.30	*Anchored off Bray.* Embarked 900 British troops. Heavy air attacks and 6-inch shelling throughout the afternoon. Had to shift billet twice.
	23.30	Proceeded. Shaped course for N. Goodwin L. V.
1st June	05.00	*Arrived Ramsgate. Disembarked 800 troops.*
	08.00	Returned to Dover.

The *Sandown* was not degaussed and was ordered to remain in harbour. Volunteer officers and crew from the *Sandown* assisted in the M/S *Medway Queen.*

Total 1,861

PS Sandown at Dover 1940

PS *Sandown* was the first of the SR paddle steamers to be requisitioned by the Navy as a mine-sweeper. Her conversion had been completed before Dunkirk so she was able to take part in the evacuation of British troops from Holland, Dunkirk, Calais and Boulogne. Thereafter her duties took her into the North Sea. It was March 1946 before she was fit to resume her peacetime role, but her continued use only lasted for another nine years.

Portsmouth Record Office

Appendix Five

Passenger Traffic to and From the Isle of Wight

In response to earlier enquiry, Mr Taylor, SR, gave the following details of passengers from and to the Isle of Wight on the days shown:

		Portsmouth/Ryde		Lymington/Yarmouth	
		From Ryde	*To Ryde*	*From Yarmouth*	*To Yarmouth*
		(No.)	*(No.)*	*(No.)*	*(No.)*
July 4/1941 (Fri)		1,375	1,334	212	110
5		1,386	1,760	139	201
6	(Sun)	1,554	1,033	-	-
7		1,292	1,487	178	320
8		1,075	1,097	111	129
9		1,004	1,053	95	88
10		970	1,338	188	151
11		1,325	1,387	211	119
12		1,234	1,782	164	161
13	(Sun)	1,142	830	-	-
14		1,499	1,428	148	218
15		1,352	1,864	444	159
16		1,153	987	245	89
17		1,267	1,382	182	137
18		1,700	1,544	179	98
19		1,562	1,828	124	144
20	(Sun)	1,479	1,118	-	-
21	(Mon)	1,487	1,396	168	204
		23,856	24,468	2,708	2,028
Nov 7/1941 (Fri)		1,099	1,066	172	123
8		997	1,351	144	131
9	(Sun)	880	634	-	-
10		1,457	1,230	256	128
11		859	795	101	80
12		867	946	144	128
13		891	839	91	120
14		1,173	1,018	137	57
15		1,033	1,005	126	75
16	(Sun)	785	614	-	-
17		1,120	1,381	91	105
18		840	781	164	128
19		813	690	106	103
20		865	974	196	70
21		1,033	1,086	83	183
22		935	1,231	143	114
23	(Sun)	1,137	705	-	-
24	(Mon)	1,093	1,198	96	119
		17,877	17,544	2,051	1,664

It was pointed out that 80 per cent of the passengers are Military and Naval personnel.

Appendix Six

Lymington-Yarmouth:
Steamboat Account

Receipts

Year	1939	1940	1941	1942	1943	1944	1945
	£	£	£	£	£	£	£
Passengers	8,897	3,144	5,543	7,712	8,267	7,170	17,713
Parcels	6,422	2,926	3,588	3,102	3,531	3,860	11,254
Mails	5	6	5	6	6	6	6
Merchandise	1,562	3,243	5,076	12,372	13,623	13,481	8,856
Livestock	100	474	476	139	48	18	25
Miscellaneous	285	545	2,498	2,425	2,459	2,554	2,580
GROSS RECEIPTS	17,271	10,338	17,186	25,756	27,934	27,089	40,434

Expenditure

Year	1939	1940	1941	1942	1943	1944	1945
	£	£	£	£	£	£	£
Salaries & Wages	5,305	4,913		6,336	6,600	6,672	8,077
Fuel	1,186	899		1,514	1,582	1,385	1,437
Stores	359	271		407	408	467	664
Repairs	3,348	3,235		6,977	7,278	11,350	12,328
Insurance	312	468		301	301	331	312
Harbour Dues	208	294		378	219	399	252
General Charges	441	470		647	672	589	613
Miscellaneous	389	473		3,692	351	168	483
Transfer to or from Renewal or Suspense	4,800	6,382		2,987	6,307	6,838	8,094
TOTAL EXPENDITURE	16,348	17,405	19,673	23,239	23,718	28,199	32,260
NET RECEIPTS	+ 923	- 7,067	- 2,487	+ 2,517	+ 4,216	- 1,110	+ 8,174